Juha Kettunen

Strategic Management in Higher Education

Juha Kettunen

Strategic Management in Higher Education

Implementing Strategic Objectives

VDM Verlag Dr. Müller

Impressum/Imprint (nur für Deutschland/ only for Germany)
Bibliografische Information der Deutschen Nationalbibliothek: Die Deutsche Nationalbibliothek verzeichnet diese Publikation in der Deutschen Nationalbibliografie; detaillierte bibliografische Daten sind im Internet über http://dnb.d-nb.de abrufbar.
Alle in diesem Buch genannten Marken und Produktnamen unterliegen warenzeichen-, marken- oder patentrechtlichem Schutz bzw. sind Warenzeichen oder eingetragene Warenzeichen der jeweiligen Inhaber. Die Wiedergabe von Marken, Produktnamen, Gebrauchsnamen, Handelsnamen, Warenbezeichnungen u.s.w. in diesem Werk berechtigt auch ohne besondere Kennzeichnung nicht zu der Annahme, dass solche Namen im Sinne der Warenzeichen- und Markenschutzgesetzgebung als frei zu betrachten wären und daher von jedermann benutzt werden dürften.

Coverbild: www.ingimage.com

Verlag: VDM Verlag Dr. Müller GmbH & Co. KG
Dudweiler Landstr. 99, 66123 Saarbrücken, Deutschland
Telefon +49 681 9100-698, Telefax +49 681 9100-988
Email: info@vdm-verlag.de
Zugl.: Oulu, University of Oulu, Diss., 2009

Herstellung in Deutschland:
Schaltungsdienst Lange o.H.G., Berlin
Books on Demand GmbH, Norderstedt
Reha GmbH, Saarbrücken
Amazon Distribution GmbH, Leipzig
ISBN: 978-3-639-29995-3

Imprint (only for USA, GB)
Bibliographic information published by the Deutsche Nationalbibliothek: The Deutsche Nationalbibliothek lists this publication in the Deutsche Nationalbibliografie; detailed bibliographic data are available in the Internet at http://dnb.d-nb.de.
Any brand names and product names mentioned in this book are subject to trademark, brand or patent protection and are trademarks or registered trademarks of their respective holders. The use of brand names, product names, common names, trade names, product descriptions etc. even without a particular marking in this works is in no way to be construed to mean that such names may be regarded as unrestricted in respect of trademark and brand protection legislation and could thus be used by anyone.

Cover image: www.ingimage.com

Publisher: VDM Verlag Dr. Müller GmbH & Co. KG
Dudweiler Landstr. 99, 66123 Saarbrücken, Germany
Phone +49 681 9100-698, Fax +49 681 9100-988
Email: info@vdm-publishing.com

Printed in the U.S.A.
Printed in the U.K. by (see last page)
ISBN: 978-3-639-29995-3

Contents

I. The strategy process and levels of strategic management   5

1. Introduction   5
2. A conceptual framework – Quality assurance and strategic planning   7
3. National networked strategy – Strategies for higher education institutions   9
4. Functional national strategies – Strategies of libraries   10
5. Regional networked strategy – Regional development of higher education institutions   12
6. Institutional strategy – Strategic planning at the Turku University of Applied Sciences   13
7. Competitive strategies – Cost leadership, differentiation and focus   14
8. Functional strategy at a higher education institution – Continuing education   16
9. Conclusions   17
References   18

II. A conceptual framework to help evaluate the quality of institutional performance   24

1. Introduction   24
2. Quality assurance   25
3. Quality audits   27
4. Direction for the future   28
5. Performance evaluation   29
6. Conclusions   30
References   31

III. Bridge building for the future of the Finnish polytechnics   34

1. Introduction   34
2. Perspectives of the Balanced Scorecard   34
3. Objectives and their causal relationships   36
4. Strategic themes and the vision for the future   38
5. Conclusions   43
References   43

IV. The strategic evaluation of academic libraries   45

1. Introduction   45
2. Strategic planning of the consortium of academic libraries   46
    The strategic plan of the consortium   46
    The strategic plan of digital libraries   47
3. Balances Scorecard approach   48
    Perspectives   48
    A strategy map   49
4. Evaluation of strategic plans   50
    Customer perspective   50
    Financial perspective   51
    Internal processes perspective   52
    Learning perspective   53
5. Conclusion   54

References   54

V. Strategic planning of regional development in higher education   57

1. Introduction   57
2. Strategic planning   58
   Mission and vision   58
   Strategic themes   59
3. The Balanced Scorecard describes the strategy   60
   The perspectives of the Balanced Scorecard   60
   Strategy maps   61
4. Strategic initiatives to implement the strategy   62
   HEIs in the regions   63
   The centre for child and youth research   63
   Treatment chains in health care   64
5. Conclusions   64
References   65

VI. The collective process and memory of strategic management   67

1. Introduction   67
2. Strategic planning   68
   Mission, vision and values   68
   Strategic themes   70
3. The Balanced Scorecard communicates and implements the strategy   71
   The perspectives of the Balanced Scorecard   71
   The introduction of the Balanced Scorecard   72
   Strategy maps   73
   The strategic architecture   74
4. The Balanced Scorecard integrated into budgeting   75
   Budgeting as a process for implementing the strategy   75
   The Balanced Scorecard of the operating units   76
   Management information system   78
5. Conclusion   79
References   80

VII. Competitive strategies in higher education   83

1. Introduction   83
2. Strategic management   84
   Self-management and accountability   85
   The role of heads of departments   85
   The evaluation of strategies   86
3. Generic competitive strategies   87
   Overall cost leadership   88
   Differentiation   89
   Focus   90
4. Conclusions   90
References   91

3

VIII. The implementation of strategies in continuing education   93

1. Introduction   94
2. Strategies for continuing education   94
3. Balanced Scorecard translates the strategy into action   95
4. Strategic themes and strategy maps   97
5. The Balanced Scorecard for continuing education   99
6. Conclusions   101
References   102

I. The strategy process and levels of strategic management

1. Introduction

Strategic management and quality assurance emphasise different aspects of management and improve the performance of the organisation. Strategic planning seeks to develop the performance of an organisation to achieve strategic objectives along the route to a vision for the future. These strategic choices may lead to a fundamental breakthrough in core institutional functions and processes. Quality assurance is another approach for organisational development that provides philosophy and tools to improve the processes continuously based on planning, implementation and systematic evaluation.

The outcome of the strategy process is a strategic plan. Strategies exist at many levels and forms. National or regional networks may have either general or functional strategies. An organisation may have an overall strategy and its support services may have functional strategies. Even individuals may say they have a strategy for their careers. This study presents the strategic plans that may take different forms at various planning levels.

Quality assurance typically takes constantly smaller steps to develop processes. In many cases the quality cycle of continuous improvement is used to plan, implement, evaluate and improve such processes. Strategic planning produces strategic objectives for a better future, while the purpose of a quality assurance system is to safeguard that these objectives can be achieved. This interpretation thus integrates strategic planning into quality assurance in internal processes and information systems.

Figure 1 describes the theoretical context of the book, including the strategy process and the implementation of the strategic plan. The strategy process takes into account the environment of the institution including the education policy, regional strategies and demand for skilled labour. It also considers the strengths and weaknesses of the institution. Typically, institutions strengthen their focus areas and take into account other higher education institutions. This creates the basis for work sharing and collaboration among institutions. The strategy process produces the strategic plan, which is implemented in annual action plans. Action and results can be expected if the implementation is efficient. The efficient implementation of the strategic plan integrates the plans with the quality assurance. Management information systems help management communicate and implement the plans throughout the organisation.

The studies of opinion leaders such as OECD (2008) discuss trends and prospects among students, academic teaching staff and graduates. The OECD study examines the link between the development of the environment and higher education policy. These exploratory studies discuss trends from both a quantitative and qualitative standpoint following the grounded theory approach developed by Barney Glaser and Anselm Strauss (Strauss, 2007; Thomas & James, 2006). Data collection from several countries and regions is the first step. Key issues are extracted from the text and data. These issues are grouped to larger concepts and categories to create themes for the education policy and to make recommendations.

Figure 1. The strategy process and the implementation of the strategic plan

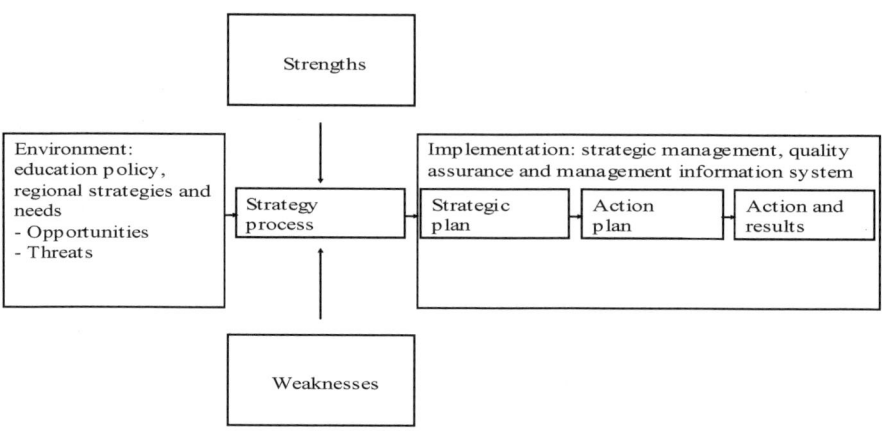

A disadvantage of the explanatory methods such as grounded theory is that it leads easily to a long list of policy recommendations. Most of them are not relevant to the strategic plan of a single higher education institution. An implication of the considerable number of recommendations is that the annual action plans of the institutions may be too ambitious and the outcomes might not be verifiable at the end of the year. The top management is pleased if only a few of the intentions are satisfactorily implemented. Many of the small changes can be implemented in a short time, but it may take 4-6 years before a new classroom practice is utilised widely enough to benefit most students, as argued by Dalin et al. (1993).

The higher education institutions can and should be managed to attain a better future and ensure high quality, but the management of higher education institutions need a framework. The objective of this study is to provide a common framework of strategic planning and quality assurance for higher education institutions. The framework does not only help management communicate and implement the strategies, but also to plan strategies in the strategy process, evaluate the performance and achievement of desired objectives and provide a structure for quality assurance and management information system. A common framework is necessary, because otherwise the evaluation of strategic management and quality assurance may be incompatible and thus compromise the success of the institution.

The common framework is based on the chapters of this book. The framework is also rigorously tested in practice. The separate sections of this chapter describe the subsequent chapters. Each section presents the main features of the strategic planning and quality assurance discussed in the chapters. The chapters provide empirical evidence for the successful implementation of the theoretical framework. The findings of this study will be useful to the administrators of educational institutions who hope to improve strategic management and quality assurance.

This book contains selected chapters on strategic management and quality assurance. The chapters are, however, samples of a larger research programme which includes many other studies in this same interest area: Kettunen (1996, 1999, 2000a,b, 2002a,b, 2003a-c, 2004a-c, 2005a-c, 2006 a,b, 2007b-d, 2008a-e, 2009b,c); Kettunen & Kantola (2006a,b, 2008a,b, 2009a) and Hautala, Kantola

& Kettunen (2009). The area of interest is supported by articles on knowledge management (Kettunen, 2009a; Kettunen, Kantola & Hautala, 2008 and Kettunen & Kulmala, 2008) and learning organisation (Kettunen, 2007a).

The various management theories discussed are related to the interest area of information and communication technology and included the following articles: Kettunen & Kantola, I (2005, 2007, 2008); Hyrkkänen, Kettunen & Putkonen (2008); Hyrkkänen, Putkonen & Kettunen (2009); Kantola, Hautala & Kettunen (2008); Kantola & Kettunen (2008); Kettunen, Hautala & Kantola (2008 a,b); Kettunen, Kantola & Hautala (2007a,b); Kettunen & Kantola (2006 a, 2007a,b) and Kettunen & Luoto (2008). These articles discuss how information systems are used to implement strategic plans and support quality assurance.

2. A conceptual framework - Quality assurance and strategic planning

The realisation of a coherent and cohesive European Higher Education Area by 2010 was agreed in the Bologna Process by the European Ministers who are responsible for higher education (Berlin Communiqué, 2003). The Ministers agreed that the national quality assurance systems of higher education should be developed and include external evaluation. The national quality assurance agencies assume responsibility for quality evaluation (Stensaker & Harvey, 2006; Filippakou & Tapper, 2007).

The Finnish Higher Education Evaluation Council and the Ministry of Education evaluate the higher education institutions. The notion of quality and quality assurance systems are not constant in the long term. There is not any well-defined framework where the targets of quality audit have been derived. The Ministry of Education has various objectives and interests derived from the education policy. These interests are highly variable based on education policy. Based on these starting points, there is clearly a need for a common and rational framework that can be used to evaluate quality and also institutional performance.

Quality assurance is a holistic approach to the development of higher education institutions. The purpose of a quality assurance system is to ensure that the strategic objectives of an institution can be achieved. That interpretation is also provided by the Finnish Higher Education Evaluation Council (2008). Quality assurance refers to the procedures, processes or systems used by an institution to safeguard and improve the quality of its education and other activities. Quality assurance is compulsory for Finnish higher education institutions. Therefore it must be taken into account in any general conceptual framework used to evaluate institutional performance.

The quality assurance system is described by using the concept of the quality map derived in this study and based on the concept of a strategy map. The quality map is a visual description for how the environment is taken into account in strategic planning (cf. OECD, 2007). It is necessary also to provide an insight into the strategic planning, management and internal processes. A great advantage of the quality map is the big picture of the quality assurance system that the map gives at first glance. Like a road map, it provides the main elements of quality assurance and helps external evaluators position minor details in a larger system.

The quality map for the Turku University of Applied Sciences includes elements of environment, strategic management and quality assurance. The environment includes global, national and regional levels. The strategic planning aspect produces a strategic plan implemented by the management process, which includes the sequence of strategic management and objectives, the planning of operations and resources, operations and steering, and finally the reporting of results. The management process is supported by the management information system tailored for each institution (Kettunen & Kantola, 2005). These internal processes are constantly monitored and improved to achieve the strategic objectives.

Strategic management is widely used in highly education institutions and cannot be avoided as these institutions are developed for a better future. Strategic management is not any management fad that fades away when new management approaches emerge. The principles of strategic management written by Sun Tzu have survived 2500 years (Sun Tzu, 2005). The Balanced Scorecard developed in the 1990s is a relatively new approach to communicate and implement the strategic plan, but the non-pecuniary indicators of the approach have been used for a very long time (Kaplan & Norton, 1992, 1993, 1996). Strategic management and the Balanced Scorecard approach are strong candidates for any general framework used to evaluate institutional performance.

The Balanced Scorecard approach divides the written strategic plan into four different perspectives: Customer, financial, internal processes and learning. Generally, these perspectives have been found to be necessary, sufficient and robust across a wide variety of organisations (Kaplan & Norton, 1996, 2001, 2004). The Balanced Scorecards of public sector organisations look remarkably similar to those developed for profit-seeking corporations. Public sector organisations place the customer at the top of the hierarchy, while private corporations emphasise the financial perspective more.

The empirical evidence supports the argument that measurement-managed organisations have better teamwork at the top, better communication throughout the organisation and better self-management at the bottom level (Lingle & Shieman, 1996). The evidence also supports that theoe organisations that use the Balanced Scorecard have been significantly more effective in comparison with other systems (Frigio & Krumwiede, 1999).

Customer perspective typically includes lagging indicators, which report on outcomes in the public sector based on activities within the internal processes perspective. In some cases, it is natural to divide the customer perspective to include both the outreach and engagement outcomes of the institution and customer satisfaction. In the case of higher education institutions, it is natural to emphasise the importance of regional development and, on the other hand, the satisfaction of students and employers.

The financial perspective is aligned with the internal processes perspective in the budgeting, and it includes the strategic objectives that must be achieved to enable the internal processes. Funding is a prerequisite for internal processes, but on the other hand, the funding perspective can emphasise the cost efficient internal processes needed to enable the sufficient funding.

The internal processes perspective describes the activities and structures of the organisation or network for which the strategy has been planned. The perspective describes the mission of the organisation along with the critical processes where the organisation must excel to finally achieve the desired outcomes in the customer perspective. Typically, the internal processes are described as a value chain, which is a sequential process moving from left to right on the strategy map.

The learning perspective describes the competence required to facilitate the internal processes and deliver future performance. These capabilities and intangible assets are drivers that may be much more important than financial accounting indicators in many information age organisations. The learning and financial perspectives indicate the resources of higher education institutions and the future events within the internal processes. Investment in the capabilities of personnel can have long-term effects on sustaining future development.

The Balanced Scorecard approach provides a general framework for understanding the causal chains between the strategic objectives placed in the perspectives. The defined causal chains between these strategic objectives can be based on either research, experience or hypotheses. The financial and learning perspectives include the drivers, while the customer perspective includes the outcomes. The strategy map presented in this study extends the conceptual framework presented by Goddard & Chatterton (2003) and the OECD (2007).

The general strategy map presented in this study is flexible enough to allow individual higher education institutions to build their own strategy maps. The desired outcomes from the region and customer perspective include strategic objectives "skills", "culture community and sustainability" and "innovation". These objectives are achieved through the internal processes, which include the objectives "R&D", "service to community" and "education". The objectives in the financial perspective are "funding from a central government", "external funding" and "cost efficiency". These objectives must be aligned with the internal processes in the budgeting. The learning perspective has drivers for the internal processes. The strategic objectives for the learning perspective are "R&D capabilities" and "teacher capabilities".

As a result of a conceptual framework for quality assurance, this study presents the auditing targets for Finland, taking into account the existing auditing targets for the Finnish Higher Education Evaluation Council. These suggestions may be valuable when the new auditing manual is planned. Another useful result of this study is that it describes the general structure of the performance indicators for Finnish universities of applied sciences. These can be used as a model when higher education institutions plan their own strategic plans, objectives and indicators or when the performance of an institution is evaluated.

3. National networked strategy - Strategies for higher education institutions

The Balanced Scorecard approach was planned for communication and implementation of the strategic plan. This study argues that the approach can also be used in strategic planning. The Balanced Scorecard approach helps management see in the planning stage what elements the strategic plan should have and what kind of structure the strategic plan should take to favour both efficient communication and implementation of the strategic plan.

There are 20 traditional science universities and 26 universities of applied sciences in Finland at the moment. The science universities have a research orientation and the universities of applied sciences have a professional orientation. Until the end of 2005, the universities of applied sciences were known as polytechnics. The strategic plan of this study was prepared for the polytechnics at the general meetings of the Rector's Conference of Finnish Polytechnics in 2003.

A strategic plan of this kind helps the Rector's Conference to influence education policy, one purpose of the Conference. The networked strategic plan also helps the institutions, which can use the plan as a basis to develop their own institutional strategic plans, action plans and scorecards that describe how they can deliver output to implement the national networked strategic plan.

When the networked strategy for the Finnish polytechnics was planned, each autonomous institution was able to align its own strategy with the national strategy. Each institution could define its own strategic themes and objectives in its own strategic plan. This process is necessary because each institution has its own environment, structure and organisational culture. Many of the Finnish polytechnics have adopted the Balanced Scorecard approach, as it helps them communicate and implement the strategic plan.

Strategic themes are important elements of the networked strategy because they can easily be used to influence national education policy. Strategic themes reflect what the rectors and the owners of the institutions believe must be done to achieve the strategic objectives. Also, the vision is an important element of the plan, because strategy is a matter of mapping the route for the better future defined by the vision (Wheale, 1991; West-Burnham, 1994). During the process, it was considered that the mission statement and values are not needed, because they are useful concepts primarily at the institutional level.

The strategy process refers to the manner and style in which the actions for a better future are planned. The sufficient interaction and communication in the strategy process strengthen the commitment to a common strategy and both aspects may be more important than the written plan itself. Altogether, 53 rectors and representatives of the owners actively participated in the strategy process to achieve a mutual understanding based on the dialogue between the planning teams selected, according to the perspectives of the Balanced Scorecard.

The Balanced Scorecard approach is a safeguard wherein the strategic objectives and causal linkages between the objectives can be described and implemented in a balanced manner, and all the necessary objectives are included in the plan. For example, the increase in the external effects and the satisfaction of students and employers are results from applied research, development and education. These achievements require a correct allocation of funding and capabilities to perform the necessary activities.

The strategic plan was presented in May 2003 to a broad audience at the General Meeting of Finnish Polytechnics, where representatives from the most important stakeholders offered valuable and positive comments. The strategic plan was published in Korkeakoulutieto Magazine of the Finnish Ministry of Education (Kettunen, 2004a). The results of the strategy process were also communicated to an international audience (Kettunen, 2004b).

An ex-post examination of the strategy process provides evidence that the strategic plan has actually driven change. The strategy process influenced the definition of the applied research and development in the new Act of Finnish Polytechnics in 2003. The strategic plan also clearly supported the establishment of second cycle degrees in 2005. In addition, the rectors of the polytechnics used the networked strategy as a basis to formulate their own institutional strategic plans.

4. Functional national strategies – Strategies of libraries

The consortium of libraries for the Finnish universities of applied sciences provides an example of the functional networked strategic plans, which supports the cooperation of otherwise independent organisational units. It is reasonable to plan strategies for the network because no single organisational unit has complete control of these libraries. This study argues that the Balanced Scorecard approach can be used to evaluate strategic plans and performance from different perspectives.

The establishment of professional-oriented Finnish universities of applied sciences at the beginning of the 1990s led to a rapid development of the libraries. There are about 500 people working in these libraries, which are located in 80 towns and at 200 locations. These facts clearly indicate the need for networked and cost efficient cooperation. The consortium of libraries (Amkit Consortium) was founded in 2001 to coordinate the full cooperation of libraries.

The consortium of libraries is a network used to gain commitment to the joint strategy as well as exchange information and cooperate. Much of the success of the libraries lies outside the given library that resides in the networked cooperation and its host institution. The informal communities of practice of the national networks and institutional teams have an essential role to play in the exchange of information and knowledge (Kettunen, 2004b; Kettunen & Kantola, 2006a).

The networked libraries prepared 2006 strategic plans for the consortium of libraries and Web service. The strategic plans are examples of fruitful cooperation of functional organisational units. The strategic plans aim to increase synergies between libraries and achieve cost efficiency. The example of libraries presented in this study can also be applied to other functions of the various support services at higher education institutions.

The libraries seek efficient ways to produce high quality output, given their shoestring financial resources. Cost efficiency is a natural choice for strategy in the public sector where taxpayers provide the financial resources for limited annual budgets. Cost efficiency can be achieved through cooperation between the libraries and taking advantage of economy of scale across both the physical and intellectual assets of the libraries.

National development teams were nominated for the main development areas. Then each library defined its own strategic themes and objectives. The libraries were able to align their budgets and human resources with the processes of the libraries to achieve their strategic objectives. The action plan of each library described how development work and processes deliver output to implement the networked strategy. Encouragement and additional funding of the Ministry of Education maintained sufficient coherence and ensured that the objectives of the consortium were achieved.

The consortium has many cooperative projects in its action plan and the action plans of the institutions. The projects include the acquisition and implementation of the Endeavor's Voyager library system (Guy, 2000; Pace, 2004; Breeding, 2006), the development of the library portal, the consortium licences of electronic acquisitions, quality management, public relations and communications and information skills studies and virtual learning environments. The consortium includes development teams for pedagogical development, e-material and facilities.

The experiences of the individual libraries support the argument that networked cooperation has been successful and provided value added for the libraries that would not have been possible by just using the resources of single libraries. The proper strategy process across the libraries, financial resources and knowledge about the development of libraries is essential for a successful networked strategy.

The strategic planning and management of networks are typically less developed than the planning of organisations and organisational units because the organisations prepare detailed budgets and human resource plans. In addition, organisations typically define indicators and set target values for the planning period. The management of the network is much more challenging than the management of the organisation because in a proper organisation, the organisational culture is much stronger, and management has the authority to make decisions.

The results of this study support the argument that the Balanced Scorecard approach provides a useful tool for evaluating strategic plans. Even though the strategic plan was not in the first place been planned using the Balanced Scorecard approach, the plan can be described using the strategy map to describe the strategic objectives and their causal relationships clearly. In addition, the strategic plan can be evaluated using the perspectives of the Balanced Scorecard. The approach is a safeguard that allows the strategic plan to be implemented in a balanced manner.

5. Regional networked strategy – Regional development of higher education institutions

According to a request by the Finnish Ministry of Education, the higher education institutions planned regional strategies in their regions. The initiative by the Ministry brought together seven higher education institutions in Southwest Finland. The initiative can be seen as a systematic approach to the utilisation of scarce resources. The institutions planned their network strategies with representatives from the City of Turku, The Regional Council of Southwest Finland and various other regional organisations. The strategic plans were approved in 2002 and 2005.

The concept of clusters introduced by Michael Porter (1990, 1996, 1998) provides a suitable basis for the network strategies of regional development because clusters are geographic concentrations of interconnected organisations in particular fields that cooperate, but may also compete. The most prominent clusters in Southwest Finland vary over economic fluctuations and planning periods, but biotechnology, information and communication technology, metal and maritime industry have held onto their strong positions during this decade.

The higher education institutions are committed to promoting the knowledge and high technology in the main clusters of the region where increased economic growth and welfare are expected. The Balanced Scorecard approach is clearly suitable for planning regional strategies because the customer perspective can be developed to take into account regional development. The regional development or outreach and engagement activities can technically be strategic objectives or alternatively the customer perspective can be divided into regional development and customer satisfaction, including student and employer satisfaction. This study argues that the Balanced Scorecard approach is ideal to describe the strategic plan even though the approach has not been used in the planning of the strategy.

Many objectives are likely to be achievable by combining the resources of the various institutions, but are unlikely if each institution operates independently. The value added gain of regional cooperation for students is to provide them a broader supply of courses and promote their employment opportunities. Typically, teachers tailor their courses to meet the needs of the region and are able to fill study groups with students from the neighbouring institution. It is likely that the cooperation of institutions does produce a better labour force for employers if the students are able to choose courses that are useful for them.

The study supports the argument that any cooperation of higher education institutions in a geographic area should be based on the strengths of institutions. Another argument is that such cooperation should be based on sharing of work and avoiding overlapping activities. The regional cooperation helps the institutions achieve cost efficiency as an outgrowth of large-scale operation, which releases resources to strengthen the strengths of institutions and increase their quality level.

Cost reductions can result from working in larger study groups, especially in basic lecture-based courses.

Research and development is another field of cooperation, where partners in projects benefit from networks and collaboration. Customer-oriented rescarch and development projects are typically multi-disciplinary and favour cross-institutional projects. Research staff typically work together on these teams to benefit from each other's knowledge and create innovations for the working life. Most of the funding bodies favour cross-institutional and demand-oriented research and development projects.

Typically, the strategy takes into account the opportunities and threats of the environment and is planned to take into account the strengths and weaknesses of the organisation to meet these external needs. The regional strategies of higher education institutions represent a class of strategies, where the strategy does not correspond to the organisational structure. A general pattern used to align the strategies of otherwise independent organisations is to define general strategic themes, objectives and development projects. Then each organisation or organisational unit can set their own strategic themes, objectives and development projects. Funding and the capabilities for regional development can secure the maintenance of sufficient coherence between operating units.

6. Institutional strategy - Strategic planning at the Turku University of Applied Sciences

This section describes the case where strategy is planned for a relatively autonomous organisation, taking into account the owner of the higher education institution. The study also describes in detail how strategic planning using the Balanced Scorecard approach is aligned with budgeting, which is the main management system in most public sector organisations. The Balanced Scorecard approach has been widely used in municipalities in Finland and other countries (Askim, 2004). This section of the study demonstrates how strategic management can be integrated with traditional budgeting in the case of the City of Turku. A city is a conglomerate of quasi-independent entities, where the Turku University of Applied Sciences has more autonomy than the other administrative branches of the city.

The City of Turku owns the Turku University of Applied Sciences, which means that elected officials hold a strong position in the ongoing decision-making of the institution. Therefore, the strategic plan of the institution must be aligned with the owner to create synergies (cf. Collis & Montgomery, 1998). The mission, vision, values and strategic themes of the institution should support upper level organisation. Another important aspect of this kind of close cooperation is that the budgeting for the City of Turku is also applied to the Turku University of Applied Sciences.

The strategic architecture of the City of Turku consists of an overall strategic plan and strategic plans of four shared support units, 22 operating units and 8 municipal companies. These units defined their Balanced Scorecards and included the main indicators in their budgets. The purpose of the strategic architecture is to have the activities of the administrative branches aligned and linked together to support the overall strategy and enable the city to implement its own strategy. The budgets with selected measures are annually approved by the City Council. In this way, employees and units are more able to see how they can contribute to the strategic objectives and the overall strategic plan for the city.

Budgeting is operational management that helps managers with tactical matters. Managers review operating performance against budgets and constantly take corrective actions. Budgets emphasise the control of costs and short-term operational details. It can be seen that another purpose of budgets is to allocate resources to strategic initiatives and achieve strategic objectives in the long run. Hence, these two lines of budgeting typically emphasise the cost efficiency and focus strategies in the public sector. Budgeting sets financial targets, but the Balanced Scorecard expands traditional budgeting to other perspectives.

The managers who are responsible must drill the strategic plan down into action plans, which describe the human resources, tasks and timetables of the organisational units. The managers have the duty of monitoring and supervision, which are essential elements of the periodic review process. The achievement of strategic objectives and performance targets is reported three times a year in the case of the Turku University of Applied Sciences.

It became evident at the Turku University of Applied Sciences that it is important to develop a management information system that supports the management process in an organisation with several organisational levels (Kettunen & Kantola, 2005). The data warehouse collects information from various data sources and provides information to the users of the management portal. The management information system is also a platform that includes budgets and human resource plans and builds an organisational memory (Nonaka & Takeuchi, 1995; Takeuchi & Nonaka, 2004).

The management information system supports the implementation of the strategic plan and the management process. It is also part of the quality assurance system of an institution. Operational management evaluates achievement of the strategic objectives and target measures using the information system. Based on the evaluation of the organisational units managers are expected to identify the goals of development and set timetables and allocate resources. Achievement of the goals described in the action plan is discussed and agreed during internal target discussions. The management information system provides evidence to external auditors on institutional quality assurance.

7. Competitive strategies - Cost leadership, differentiation and focus

The heads of departments in higher education institutions are in a key position to plan the future direction of their sub-units. They can also contribute to the overall strategy of the institution. A higher education institution typically has many sub-units, which do not necessarily follow the same competitive strategy. This study shows that the strategies of cost leadership, differentiation and focus, which were developed for business companies by Porter (1990), can successfully be applied in the public sector. The overall strategic plan can be translated into more diversified strategies of sub-units. This procedure is especially appropriate for market-led continuing education, which operates in a competitive market and is also different from degree programmes.

Cost efficiency is based on internal processes that rely on scale economies in facility management, the sizes of study groups, support services and functional policies. This strategy requires the pursuit of cost reductions in areas not in the primary focus field of the organisation. A low-cost position requires product development and a great deal of managerial attention to keep costs low. Cost efficiency is necessary in the highly competitive markets of continuing education where the price level is low.

Labour market training is a typical example where cost leadership strategy is relevant because competition between the education institutions arranged by the funding body forces the winner of such competition to bid the lowest price. Another example is the Open University, which operates in a cost efficient manner. The courses can be easily planned, because the Open University is able to teach paying customers the same courses as the faculty teaches degree students. Another method of cost efficiency is to arrange joint courses with faculties. An advantage of both these examples is that the continuing education centre and the Open University have favourable access to faculty teachers. The cost leadership strategy does not mean that the courses are significantly better than others, but that they have sufficient quality level.

A differentiation strategy can be applied if the organisational unit wants to differentiate itself from others by using various dimensions. A strong brand image, advanced technology, excellent customer service or other dimensions can be used to make the unit different in the eyes of customers. The primary target of the unit is to create an image that is unique in educational markets. This strategy is typically mixed with the focus strategy, but that choice does not mean that costs are completely ignored.

The Executive Master of Business Administration (MBA) programme is a typical example of educational programmes that follow the differentiation strategy. The educational programme has a strong brand known all over the world. The successful managers of the Executive MBA programmes select students carefully, accepting only those who create added value for peer learning. The Executive MBA programmes typically have the best lectures in the country, intensive courses abroad and take good care of customers, all of which are crucial in attracting high-income business managers to this expensive education and maintaining a perception of exclusivity (Kettunen, 1999, 2000a,b). There are many other degrees which also have strong educational brands.

The focus strategy has a primary target, where it selects a particular customer segment from the market. The segment may be a geographic market, occupation group or organisational level. The service or product is tailored to meet the needs of the customer segment. The purpose is to serve the particular customer very well. The focus strategy rests on the assumption that it is more profitable to serve a narrow customer segment well than operate in broad markets. As a result of the focus strategy, the organisation will also become different from others or achieve lower costs. The focus strategy has a trade-off between profitability and sales volume, which is the strategic choice of top management.

The Finnish universities of applied sciences typically focus on profession-oriented education, whereas traditional science universities focus on subject-oriented education. Therefore, the focus strategy is a natural choice for profession-oriented education. The focus strategy may, however, mean reducing the number of customers. This strategy can lead to a close customer relationship where the service provider has only one customer. For example, Jollas Instituutti and K-insituutti serve only certain large retail companies in Finland.

Three generic competitive strategies are alternative strategic choices. Any organisation failing to develop its strategy, in at least one of these directions, is probably guaranteed to be unsuccessful. An organisation stuck in the middle of these strategies will be unable to make clear choices and define its strategic objectives. The effective implementation of the strategic plan requires a clear strategic choice and supporting arrangements. If the sub-units of the large organisation are clearly different from each other, each can pursue different competitive strategies. This choice is especially relevant in the case of continuing education.

8. Functional strategy at a higher education institution - Continuing education

Finnish higher education institutions have continuing education centres or special units of faculties. This section describes the functional strategy of the continuing education centre of the Turku University of Applied Sciences, which was known as Turku Polytechnic until the end of 2005. During the study Turku Polytechnic had nine education departments (faculties), support services and a continuing education centre. The role of the continuing education centre was to manage continuing education while the faculties provided most of the teachers for continuing education.

The strategy of the continuing education centre represents the functional strategy of the entire organisation. The basic strategic alternatives for the centre are cost leadership, differentiation and focus where the centre provides a unique mix of service for its customers (cf. Treacy & Wiersema, 1995). Turku University of Applied Sciences chose the focus strategy combined with the strategy of cost leadership as its general overall strategy.

The continuing education centre developed and refined the chosen overall strategy. The centre is operating in a competitive market where it has a trade-off between profitability and sales volume. The strictly selected market segments, according to the focus strategy, emphasise profitability, but on the other hand, the larger market segments emphasise growth. The continuing education centre aims to keep the financial result positive in its budget. Therefore, the centre redefined its strategy by aiming for profitable growth.

The selected strategy allows for a customer-intimate education, providing an excellent combination of costs and quality in education. The geographic area of Southwest Finland and its main clusters are the broad focus areas. The other focus is a profession-oriented education, which is typical of Finnish universities of applied sciences. An obvious reason for choosing the cost efficiency strategy is the fact that each educational programme has unit-priced funding stipulated by the central government or the price of education as defined in the competitive markets.

The strategic plan is written in a concise form, using a small number of strategic themes. Often the strategic plans are long written documents where essential elements are difficult to identify without basic strategic themes. They reflect what management believes must be done to achieve the vision and its more detailed strategic objectives. Strategic themes are linked with the strategic objectives and create dynamic tension between them. Each organisation has a unique set of strategic themes that remain typically unchanged during the planning period.

The strategic plan is presented in a graphical form, using the strategy map, which is developed for the case of continuing education. The objectives presented on the strategy map are balanced into perspectives and transformed into strategic objectives. The strategy map helps management understand the causal linkages between the objectives and implement the plan effectively. The strategy map helps staff understand precisely why specific targets have been set for the planning period.

The desired strategic objectives are "regional development" and "customer satisfaction". These objectives can be achieved by the sequential process of a value chain that included the objectives of "research and development", "support services" and "education". The prerequisites for these objectives are "external funding" and "funding from the central government" in the financial perspective and "the capability for R&D", "environmental scanning and customer knowledge" and "quality and assessment capabilities, and in-house training" in the learning and growth perspective.

The numerical Balanced Scorecard was developed to help management communicate important measures to staff and external stakeholders and effectively implement the strategic plan. The Balanced Scorecard translates objectives in the perspectives into tangible measurements. The measurement system should indicate the causal relationships between performance drivers and outcome measures, customised to the strategic themes. The target values of indicators are agreed upon the planning period during the internal target negotiations between top management and departments and then annually checked for whether the action plan contains sufficient elements to achieve the target values.

The indicators of the Balanced Scorecard should describe the achievement of strategic objectives. Therefore, only a relatively small number of indicators are needed. The indicators have to be simple and understandable for both management and staff. They should not place any extra burdens on the people responsible for data collection. The Finnish AMKOTA files of the Finnish universities of applied sciences provide a good basis for these indicators, because the data are collected on a regular basis and support clear comparisons to other higher education institutions.

The strategy of cost leadership has been successful. The statistics produced by The Finnish National Board of Education indicate that the administrative costs of the Turku University of Applied Sciences are the lowest in the country. In addition, the average costs of support services are about 20 per cent higher in other institutions (http://vos.uta.fi/rap/kust/v07/k04z6la.html). Effective administration and support services leave more resources available for education and applied research and development, which are of course the main activities of the institution.

9. Conclusions

The case studies described by chapters show that the Balanced Scorecard approach can be used for strategies of various kinds at different levels of planning. At the national level, the study presents a network strategy of the universities of applied sciences and the functional strategic plans of their libraries. At the regional level, the study presents a network strategy of higher education institutions and the strategy of the Turku University of Applied Sciences as part of the strategy of the City of Turku. At the institutional level, the study presents competitive strategies, which are applied in continuing education.

In the context of the strategy process, the management must have proper tools to prepare the strategic plan. This study argues that the Balanced Scorecard is not only a tool for communicating and implementing the strategic plan, but also an approach to plan strategies in a way that takes all perspectives into account, defines clear strategic objectives, assumes causal relationships among the objectives, and defines strategic themes describing what management believes must be done in order to achieve the desired outcomes.

In relation to quality assurance, the study argues that the Balanced Scorecard can be used to evaluate the performance of an institution and the achievement of its strategic objectives. Evaluation of higher education institutions and their activities is easily random, inaccurate and uncertain if there is no common framework to evaluate the institutions. A common framework helps evaluators avoid misinterpretations and erroneous conceptions. An accurate evaluation helps the institution in enhancement led evaluations to select the right remedies and continuously improve.

The role of the top management is to lead the strategy process. Often the strategy process produces a plan which is not easy to interpret. The strategic plan must be understandable to the managers and staff before it can be implemented. The top management must also provide their managers and members of the staff with tools for communicating and implementing the strategic plan. The strategic plan must be described by strategic themes and divided into different perspectives and strategic objectives before it can be implemented. There must be sufficient funding and knowledge for the efficient internal processes, which provide the external effects and produce satisfied customers.

The Balanced Scorecard is useful in the planning of the management information system. The structure of the management information system was planned at the Turku University of Applied Sciences to support the management process, which is based on strategic management and the Balanced Scorecard approach. The action plan of the management information system integrates the quality assurance and the implementation of the strategic plan. The system was tailored to the institution, because the organisation is different from the other institutions. The experiences of the system confirm that the Balanced Scorecard approach is capable of translating the strategic plan into objectives and tangible measures for the planning period.

The Balanced Scorecard approach has been applied and tested in several settings. An advantage of the approach is that all the strategic objectives can be aligned in budgeting with the financial objectives. In this respect, the approach extends the traditional pecuniary measures to real economy. The budget and human resources and action plans constitute an ensemble of documents, which reflect the implementation of the strategic plan. The Balanced Scorecard approach is flexible, because it can be used to apply various kinds of competitive strategies.

References

Askim, J. (2004). Performance management and organizational intelligence: Adapting the Balanced Scorecard in Larvik Municipality, International Public Management Journal, 7(3), 415-438.

Berlin Communiqué (2003). Bologna Process Berlin 2003, Realising the European higher education area, Communiqué of the conference of Ministers responsible for higher education in Berlin on 19 September 2003.

Breeding, M. (2006). Reshuffling the deck, Library Journal, Retrieved 28th October, 2006, from http://www.libraryjournal.com/article/CA6319048.html.

Collis, D. and Montgomery, C. (1998). Creating corporate advantage, Harvard Business Review, May-June, 70-83.

Dalin, P., Roff, H. and Kleekamp, B. (1993). Changing the school culture. London: Cassell.

Johnson, G. and Scholes, K. (1993). Exploring corporate strategy. Hemel Hempstead: Prentice-Hall.

Guy, F. (2000). Progress towards the development of digital libraries: The experiences of some national libraries in North America, Australasia and Europe, Russian Digital Libraries Journal, 3(3), Retrieved 28th October, 2006, from http://www.elbib.ru/index.phtml?page=elbib/eng/journal/2000/part3/guy.

Filippakou, O. and Tapper, T. (2007). Quality assurance in higher education: Thinking beyond the English experience, Higher Education Policy, 20(3), 339-360.

Finnish Higher Education Evaluation Council (2008). Audits of quality assurance systems of Finnish higher education institutions, Audit manual for 2008-2011, Finnish Higher Education Evaluation Council 10:2007, Retrieved 20th March 2008, from http://www.kka.fi/pdf/julkaisut/KKA_1007.pdf.

Frigio, M.L. and Krumwiede, K. (1999). Balanced Scorecard: A rising trend in strategic performance measurement, Journal of Strategic Performance Measurement, February-March, 42-48.

Goddard, J.B. and Chatterton, P. (2003). The response of universities to regional needs, In Boekema, F., Kuypers, E. and Rutten, R. (eds.), Economic Geography of Higher Education: Knowledge, Infrastructure and Learning Regions. London: Routledge, 19-41.

Hautala, J., Kantola, M. and Kettunen, J. (2009). Challenges of multidisciplinary and innovative learning, Teachers and Teaching: Strategies, Innovations and Problem Solving. Hauppauge, NY: Nova Science Publishers, accepted for publication.

Hyrkkänen, U., Kettunen, J. and Putkonen, A. (2008). A participatory design project on mobile ICT, In Cartelli, A. and Palma, M. (eds.), Encyclopedia of Information Communication Technology. Hershey, PA: IGI Global, 669-675.

Hyrkkänen, U., Putkonen, A. and Kettunen, J. (2009). Complexity and work load factors in virtual work environment of mobile work, In Khosrow-Pour, M. (ed.), Encyclopedia of Information Science and Technology. Hershey, PA: IGI Global, 634-640.

Kantola, M., Hautala, J. and Kettunen, J. (2008). Electronic joint application system in higher education, International Journal of e-Business Management, 2(1), 39-50.

Kantola, M. and Kettunen, J. (2008). Service-oriented architecture in higher education, In Tomei, L.A. (ed.), Encyclopedia of Information Technology Curriculum Integration, Hershey, PA: IGI Global, 751-757.

Kaplan, R. and Norton, D. (1992). The Balanced Scorecard - Measures that drive performance, Harvard Business Review, January-February, 71-79.

Kaplan, R. and Norton, D. (1993). Putting the Balanced Scorecard to work, Harvard Business Review, September-October, 134-147.

Kaplan, R. and Norton, D. (1996). The Balanced Scorecard. Boston, MA: Harvard Business School Press.

Kaplan, R. and Norton, D. (2001). The strategy-focused organization. Boston, MA: Harvard Business School Press.

Kaplan, R. and Norton, D. (2004). Strategy maps. Boston, MA: Harvard Business School Press

Kettunen, J. (1996). Yritysjohtajien näkemyksiä kansantaloutemme kuntoon saattamisesta (Views of executives on reshaping the Finnish economy), The Finnish Journal of Business Economics, 4/1996, 419-429.

Kettunen, J. (1999). Customer recommendations for MBA programmes, International Journal: Continuous Improvement Monitor, 1(4), 1-13.

Kettunen, J. (2000a). Individual and in-house MBA programmes, In Boonchaoy, A., Kiokaew, S., Sinprajukpol, W. and Gearter, A.F. (eds.), Proceedings of the International Symposium on A Blueprint for Better Graduate Studies, Grad-Blue Print 2000, Graduate School, Prince of Songkla University, Thailand, 238-253.

Kettunen, J. (2000b). Management education and organization development, In Tøsse, S., Falkencrone, P., Puurula, A. and Bergstedt, B. (eds.), Reforms and Policy, Adult Education Research in Nordic Countries. Trondheim: Tapir Academic Press, 143-159.

Kettunen, J. (2002a). Competitive strategies in higher education, Journal of Institutional Research, 11(2), 38-47.

Kettunen, J. (2002b). Demand for continuing education of managers, The Finnish Journal of Business Economics, 2/2002, 145-156.

Kettunen, J. (2003a). Professional development in public administration, Pakistan Journal of Social Sciences, 1(2), 74-79.

Kettunen, J. (2003c). The length of study of MBA students, International Journal of Lifelong Education, 22(2), 159-171.

Kettunen, J. (2003c). Strategic evaluation of institutions by students in higher education, Perspectives: Policy & Practice in Higher Education, 7(1), 14-18.

Kettunen, J. (2004a). Ammattikorkeakoulujen strategia ohjaa toimintaa, Korkeakoulutieto 2/2004, Ministry of Education, Finland, 20-25.

Kettunen, J. (2004b). Bridge building for the future of Finnish polytechnics, Journal of Higher Education Outreach and Engagement, 9(2), 43-57.

Kettunen, J. (2004c). The strategic evaluation of regional development in higher education, Assessment & Evaluation in Higher Education, 29(3), 357-368.

Kettunen, J. (2005a). Business plans for continuing education, Pakistan Journal of Social Sciences, 3(1), 43-48.

Kettunen, J. (2005b). Implementation of strategies in continuing education, The International Journal of Educational Management, 19(3), 207-217.

Kettunen, J. (2005c). The centre for mechanical engineering – A development and learning environment for the cooperation of educational institutions and companies, Learning the skills, Special Edition of the Finnish Journal of Vocational and Professional Education, 45-53.

Kettunen, J. (2006a). Strategies for the cooperation of educational institutions and companies in mechanical engineering, The International Journal of Educational Management, 20(1), 19-28.

Kettunen, J. (2006b). Strategic planning of regional development in higher education, Baltic Journal of Management, 1(3), 259-269.

Kettunen, J. (2007a). Innovativeness in higher education management, Bhavishya, Journal of Future Business School, 1(2), 65-74.

Kettunen, J. (2007b). Strategies for the cooperation of higher educational institutions in ICT, In Rahman, H. (ed.) Information and Communication Technologies for Economic and Regional Developments. Hershey, PA: Idea Group Publishing, 22-38.

Kettunen, J. (2007c). Strategies of regional development, In Ghosh, A. and Banerjee, G. (eds.), Strategic Management for Firms in Developing Countries. New Delhi: Allied Publishers, 520-530.

Kettunen, J. (2007d). The strategic evaluation of academic libraries, Library Hi Tech, 25(3), 409-421.

Kettunen, J. (2008a). A conceptual framework to help evaluate the quality of institutional performance, Quality Assurance in Education, 16(4), 322-332.

Kettunen, J. (2008b). Creating the European Higher Education Area – An institutional perspective, In Larkey, J.E. and Maynhard, V.B. (eds.), Innovation in Education. Hauppauge, NY: Nova Science Publishers, 207-218.

Kettunen, J. (2008c). Human resources in the Balanced Scorecard system, In Torres-Coronas, T. and Arias-Oliva, M. (eds.), Encyclopedia of Human Resources Information Systems: Challenges in e-HRM. Hershey, PA: IGI Global, 464-470.

Kettunen, J. (2008d). Management information system in higher education, In Cartelli, A. and Palma, M. (eds.), Encyclopedia of Information Communication Technology. Hershey, PA: IGI Global, 542-547.

Kettunen, J. (2008e). Strategies for virtual organizations, In Putnik, G.D. and Cunha, M.M. (eds.), Encyclopedia of Networked and Virtual Organisations. Hershey, PA: IGI Global, 1528-1534.

Kettunen, J. (2009a). Construction of knowledge-intensive organization in higher education. Handbook of Research on Knowledge-Intensive Organizations. Hershey, PA: IGI Global, 19-29.

Kettunen, J. (2009b). The collective process and memory of strategic management, In Girard, J.P. (ed.), Building Organizational Memories: Will You Know What You Knew? Hershey, PA: IGI Global, 148-163.

Kettunen, J. (2009c). The strategic plan of digital libraries in higher education, In Theng, Y.-L., Foo, S., Goh, D. and Na, J.-C. (eds.), Handbook of Research on Digital Libraries. Hershey, PA: IGI Global, 457-464.

Kettunen, J., Hautala, J. and Kantola, M. (2008a). Dynamic information systems in higher education, Encyclopedia of Multimedia Technology and Networking. Hershey, PA: IGI Global, 430-435.

Kettunen, J., Hautala, J. and Kantola, M. (2008b). Information environments of middle managers in higher education, In Cartelli, A. and Palma, M. (eds.), Encyclopedia of Information Communication Technology. Hershey, PA: IGI Global, 436-442.

Kettunen, J. and Kantola, I. (2005). Management information system based on the Balanced Scorecard, Campus-Wide Information Systems, 22(5), 263-274.

Kettunen, J. and Kantola, I. (2007). E-collaboration of quality assurance in higher education, In Khosrow-Pour, M. (ed.), Managing Worldwide Operations and Communications with Information Technology. Hershey, PA: IGI Global, 1089-1092.

Kettunen, J. and Kantola, I. (2008). Quality assurance view of a management information system, In Cartelli, A. and Palma, M. (eds.), Encyclopedia of Information Communication Technology. Hershey, PA: IGI Global, 691-697.

Kettunen, J. and Kantola, M. (2006a). Strategies for virtual learning and e-entrepreneurship, In Zhao, F. (ed.), Entrepreneurship and Innovations in E-Business: An Integrative Perspective. Hershey, PA: Idea Group Publishing, 107-123.

Kettunen, J. and Kantola, M. (2006b). The implementation of the Bologna Process, Tertiary Education and Management, 12(3), 257-267.

Kettunen, J. and Kantola, M. (2007). Strategic planning and quality management in the Bologna Process, Perspectives, Policy and Practice in Higher education, 11(3), 67-73.

Kettunen, J., Kantola, M. and Hautala, J. (2007a). An academic management portal, In Tatnall, A. (ed.), Encyclopedia of Portal Technology and Applications. Hershey, PA: IGI Global, 1-5

Kettunen, J., Kantola, M. and Hautala, J. (2007b). E-management portal and organisational behaviour, In Tatnall, A. (ed.), Encyclopedia of Portal Technology and Applications. Hershey, PA: IGI Global, 316-320.

Kettunen, J., Kantola, M. and Hautala, J. (2008). Knowledge management with partners in a dynamic information environment, In Cartelli, A. and Palma, M. (eds.), Encyclopedia of Information Communication Technology. Hershey, PA: IGI Global, 503-509.

Kettunen, J. and Kulmala, R. (2008). Intellectual property protection in software enterprises, In Pagani, M. (ed.), Encyclopedia of Multimedia Technology and Networking. Hershey, PA: IGI Global, 697-702.

Kettunen, J. and Luoto, L. (2008). Cooperation between universities and ICT enterprises, In Zhao, F. (ed.), Handbook of Research on Information Technology Entrepreneurship and Innovation. Hershey. PA: IGI Global, 277-292.

Lingle, J.H. and Shieman, W.A. (1996). From Balanced Scorecards to strategic gauges: Is measurement worth it? Management Review, March, 56-62.

Nonaka, I. and Takeuchi, H. (1995). The knowledge-creating company. New York: Oxford University Press.

OECD (2007). Higher education and regions, Globally competitive, locally engaged, Organisation for Economic Co-operation and Development. Paris: OECD Publishing.

OECD (2008). Higher education to 2030, Volume 1, Demography. Paris: OECD Publishing.

Pace, A.K. (2004). Dismantling integrated library systems, Library Journal, Retrieved 28th October, 2006, from http://libraryjournal.com/article/CA374953.html.

Porter, M. (1990). The competitive advantage of nations. London: MacMillan.

Porter, M. (1996). What is strategy? Harvard Business Review, November-December, 61-78.

Porter, M. (1998). On competition. Boston, MA: Harvard Business School Press.

Strauss, A. (1987). Qualitative analysis for social scientists. Cambridge: Cambridge University Press.

Stensaker, B. and Harvey, L. (2006), Old wine in new bottles? A comparison of public and private accreditation schemes in higher education, Higher Education Policy, 19(1), 65–85.

Sun Tzu, S. (2005). The Art of War, Retrieved 18th Mars, 2009, from http://www.lulu.com/items/volume_6/164000/164578/4/preview/TheArtofWarFinalVersion.pdf.

Takeuchi, H. and Nonaka, I. (2004). Hitotsubashi on knowledge management. Singapore: John Wiley & Sons.

Thomas, G. & James, D. (2006). Re-inventing grounded theory: some questions about theory, ground and discovery. British Educational Research Journal, 32 (6), 767–795.

Treacy M. and Wiersema, F. (1995). The discipline of market leaders: Choose your customers, narrow your focus, dominate your market. Reading, MA: Addison-Wesley.

West-Burnham, J. (1994). Strategy, policy and planning, In Bush, T. and West-Burnham, J. (eds.), The Principles of Educational Management. Harlow: Longman.

Wheale, J. (1991). Generating income for educational institutions: A business planning approach. London: Kogan Page.

II. Conceptual Framework to Evaluate Quality and Institutional Performance

1. Introduction

International development, particularly structural development, quality assurance and increased co-operation, present new challenges for higher education institutions (HEIs), which compete and co-operate in the global market and the European Higher Education Area. Competition and cooperation have led to a situation where trust in the standard of higher education is no longer a sufficient requisite to guarantee quality. Higher education should be transparent and credible internationally and enable student and labour mobility.

The European Ministers responsible for higher education agreed in the Bologna Process to realise a coherent and cohesive European Higher Education Area by 2010 (Berlin Communiqué, 2003). They agreed among other things that the national quality assurance systems of higher education should include external review. The national quality assurance system is usually composed of the evaluation activities of the agencies responsible for the quality evaluation (Stensaker and Harvey, 2006, Filipakou and Tapper, 2007). In addition, the Ministry of Education and many other bodies evaluate and study the quality and performance of HEIs.

The political objectives set for the future assume that there must be effective and widely used management tools at the institutional level. The future orientation of the education policy emphasises the need to define the direction and scope of the HEI in the long term. Strategic planning produces an explicit description how an organisation is moving from the present day described by the mission in the intended direction and the state expressed by the vision (Fidler, 2002, Davies and Ellison, 2003, Steiss, 2003). Strategic management matches the changing education policy and the regional circumstances to the resources of the institution.

Strategic management defines strategic objectives, which take into account the international and national educational policies and the regional demand for skilled labour. When the performance of an HEI is evaluated, the objectives of the education policy and strategic plans must be taken into account, otherwise the evaluation is not consistent with the environment of the HEI. The Balanced Scorecard approach developed by Kaplan and Norton (1996, 2001, 2004) is a widely used tool to effectively communicate and implement the strategic plan.

The successful evaluation of the institutional performance means that there must be a general and common conceptual framework to describe and evaluate the performance. The framework for evaluating the institutional performance should include the elements of the quality assurance, strategic management and the Balanced Scorecard approach. The framework for evaluating quality and institutional performance must be flexible, because the aim of the quality assurance agencies is not to harmonise the quality assurance systems according to any particular predetermined model.

The purpose of this chapter is to construct a flexible framework to evaluate the quality assurance system and institutional performance including the strategic management and internal processes of the HEI. Quality assurance must be taken into account, because it is mandatory and at the responsibility of the institution. The framework is described in this study using quality and strategy maps which can be used to describe the overall structure of the framework needed. This study presents the model which is directly applicable to the Finnish universities of applied sciences and can be modified for other HEIs.

The chapter is organised as follows: The next section introduces the concept of the quality map to describe the quality assurance system of the HEI. Then the targets of the quality audit are presented. Thereafter the general strategy map is presented including the strategic objectives and the causal linkages between the various perspectives and objectives. Based on the strategy map the criteria for the evaluation of institutional performance are presented. Finally the results of the study are summarised and discussed in the concluding section.

2. Quality assurance

Quality assurance is a holistic approach providing a philosophical framework for the development of HEIs. According to the definition of the Finnish Higher Education Evaluation Council it refers to the procedures, processes or systems used by the HEI to safeguard and improve the quality of its education and other activities (Finnish Higher Education Evaluation Council, 2008). In this study, quality assurance is seen to overlap strategic planning, because strategic planning is an essential management activity where high quality can be expected. Therefore strategic planning, management process, internal processes and systems must be taken into account in the framework to evaluate quality assurance.

As in many other countries, the Finnish HEIs are autonomous and therefore assume responsibility for their own quality assurance. Each institution builds its own quality assurance system, sets objectives and selects the methods of quality assurance. The Finnish Higher Education Evaluation Council is responsible for the external evaluation of HEIs. The external evaluation is based on the Standards and Guidelines for Quality Assurance in the European Higher Education Area (European Association for Quality Assurance in Higher Education, 2005). Quality assurance must be taken into account in the general conceptual framework to evaluate the institutional performance, because quality assurance is compulsory for HEIs.

The quality assurance system can be described using the concept of the quality map. The quality map is a visual representation how the environment is taken into account in strategic planning. It also provides an insight into the strategic planning, management process and internal processes and helps the managers, personnel, external evaluators and other stakeholders to get the big picture regarding the quality assurance system of the institution. As in the case of the road map it is easier to piece together the minor details if the main characteristics are described.

Figure 1 describes the comprehensive quality map of the Turku University of Applied Sciences (TUAS). The environment includes the global, national and regional dimensions as described in the study by the OECD (2007). The European education policy provides, to a large extent, the outlines for the global dimension of Finnish HEIs. Science and technology and industrial policy are converging towards a national innovation policy which embodies strong links with territorial development, higher education policy and labour market policy. The global dimension and national policy are mixed with the regional dimension to create of the environment of the HEI.

Strategic planning is essentially the strategy process, which produces the overall strategic plan and the objectives for the planning period. The strategy process also produces sub-strategies, which focus on the specific function of the organisation. The HEIs take the challenge of taking into account the changes in the environment and involve a sufficient number of managers and personnel in the strategy process. The participation of the regional representatives of stakeholders, students and personnel in a strategy process can be seen as more important than the final strategic plan. In knowledge-intensive work, the stakeholders and experts can commit themselves to the strategic plan more easily if they are able to contribute to it.

The management process is actually the sequence of management activities which include four sequences of management: strategic management and the updating of strategic objectives, the planning of operations and resources, the operations and steering and the reporting of results. The purpose of the operational management is to achieve the strategic objectives and continuously improve the internal processes. Management information systems have been tailored for HEIs to automate the management and measuring system. The information is typically collected from various data sources into a database and used through a management portal (Kettunen and Kantola, 2005).

In a successful case, the management process is integrated with the quality assurance system, which produces evaluative information about processes and results. The feedback and other information about the achievement of the targets are used to develop the processes. The corrective actions are determined in each process and at each institutional level. The management information system contributes to the continuous improvement and produces evidence of the corrective actions for the quality audits. If the quality assurance system is not integrated with the management system, it will remain isolated and will not yield the desired results of quality enhancement.

The main internal processes are embodied in the sequential process where the previous stages add new value to the next phases. The main internal processes include research and development (R&D), service to the community and other support services and education. These activities can be described as the cooperation between different people and organisational units in the internal processes perspective, but often they are inexplicably linked with each other. The institution needs a common strategy and action plan to better integrate its activities and create cost efficiency and competitive advantage. Each institution is responsible for its quality assurance system and therefore the quality maps may have slightly variable architectures.

Figure 1. Quality map of a higher education institution

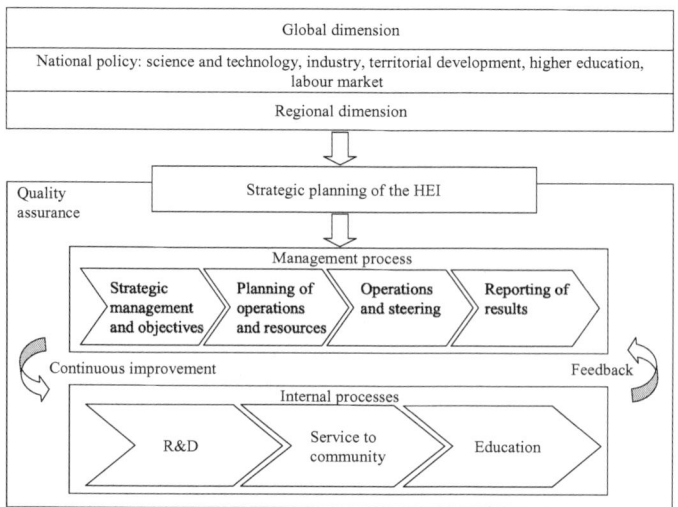

3. Quality audits

Many European countries have established quality assurance agencies and developed national quality assurance systems. They use various terms to describe their auditing procedures: the institutional audit, quality audit, the evaluation of quality assurance systems or enhancement-led institutional review. The Finnish response to the aims and objectives set in the Berlin communiqué was deliberated by a committee on quality assurance (Ministry of Education, Finland, 2004). The committee proposed that the HEIs develop quality assurance systems covering all their operations and that these be regularly evaluated by the Finnish Higher Education Evaluation Council.

The quality assurance system may refer to the environments and quality assurance systems of the international and national levels and the environment and quality assurance system of an individual HEI. The quality audits should encompass how the institution takes account of these matters in its strategic planning, management process and internal processes. On the other hand, the national aim of quality audits is to support HEIs in their quality management and performance enhancement.

Next the quality map approach is used to develop the auditing targets for Finland taking into account the auditing targets of the Finnish Higher Education Evaluation Council (2008). Following the structure of the strategy map the auditing of an HEI should include the following targets:

1. The consistency of the strategic plans with the global, national and regional environments
2. Strategic planning and objectives, overall structure and internal coherence of the strategic plans
3. Documentation of the management process including the definition of procedures, actors and responsibilities
    a) Strategic management and objectives
    b) Planning of operations and resources (financial and human)
    c) Operations and steering
    d) Reporting of results
4. Objectives, overall structure and the internal coherence of the quality assurance system
    a) Definition of the objectives, functions, actors and responsibilities of the HEI's quality assurance system as well as the respective documentation
    b) Monitoring, evaluation and continuous improvement of the quality assurance system
    c) Participation of staff, students and external stakeholders in quality assurance
    d) Relevance of, and access to, information generated by the quality assurance system within the HEI and from the perspective of the external stakeholders of the HEI
5. The comprehensiveness and effectiveness of the quality assurance procedures and structures related to the internal processes of the HEI
    a) Research and development
    b) Service to the community (the interaction with and impact on society as well as regional development cooperation) and support services (such as the library and information services, career and recruitment services and international services and staff development)
    c) Education

The approach developed in this study sorts the quality targets following the order of the quality map and enhances the role of strategic planning so that the plan is consistent with the global, national and regional environments. This is consistent with the concept of the fitness for purpose, which sees quality as fulfilling the requirements, needs and desires of customers (Harvey, 2004). The environments may be different for the different HEIs. For example, the traditional science universities produce universal knowledge for society and mankind, but the role of the universities of applied sciences is to serve their region.

This study emphasises the importance of the documentation of the management process. This is essential, because the documentation produces the audit material about the functioning of the quality assurance system. The documentation should include the strategic plans, the management process and internal processes. Action plans and course implementation plans, among others, are important documents, which provide the evidence of the continuous improvement of the quality cycle (Deming, 1986, Tague, 2004, Temponi, 2005, Houston, 2008).

The HEI involved in the audit process should collect the audit material and provide the audit group with sufficient information and evidence to assess the comprehensiveness, performance, effectiveness as well as the transparency of the quality assurance system. The HEI must compile the audit material to provide the auditors with an overview of the organisation, the quality assurance system, its links to the operative steering system and the evidence of the performance of the quality assurance system (Finnish Higher Education Evaluation Council, 2008).

4. Direction for the future

The autonomy of HEIs emphasises the need for strong management and accountability to stakeholders (Moses, 2007, Salmi, 2007). The self-regulation of institutions enhances the responsibility of HEIs to select the tools for management (Maassen and Stensaker, 2003). Strategic management is widely used in HEIs. This involves taking the holistic view of the institution in its environment and aims to map the route to the desired future situation (Kettunen, 2005, 2006a, 2007). Therefore strategic management is a strong candidate for inclusion in the framework to evaluate institutional performance.

The Balanced Scorecard approach is an efficient method for the communication and implementation of the strategic plan. The approach ensures that the strategic plan is described by strategic objectives and measures and balanced in a generic form into four different perspectives. The approach is also a guarantee that the performance of the institution and its units are directly linked to the strategic plan. Once the targets of the measures have been agreed, the precise steps can be taken and the achievement of the targets can be reviewed.

Figure 2 presents a general strategy map which is a general representation of the relationships between the strategic objectives and the perspectives of an HEI. The region and customers perspective includes the desired outcomes of the institution (Kettunen, 2004a,b, 2006b). These are the results of the internal processes, which must be aligned with financing in the budgeting process. The learning perspective includes the personnel capabilities, which are the performance drivers to achieve objectives in the internal processes. Each organisation can define its own perspectives, but these general perspectives have been found necessary and sufficient across a wide variety of organisations. The perspectives of the Balanced Scorecard approach are natural choices for the evaluation of performance, because they have been planned to communicate and implement the strategy.

The strategy map extends the conceptual framework presented by Goddard and Chatterton (2003) and the OECD (2007). The strategy map adds the financing and learning perspectives to the framework of earlier studies, but uses the same strategic objectives of "skill", "innovation" and "culture community and sustainability". The financing perspective includes the strategic objectives of "funding from central government", "external funding" and "cost efficiency". The internal processes have been described in a similar way as in the quality map because the essence of the quality and strategy is in the activities. The strategic objective "service to community" can also be extended to include the objectives of support services. The learning perspective includes the strategic objectives of "R&D capabilities" and "teacher capabilities". These personnel capabilities are prerequisites for the achievement of the strategic objectives related to the internal processes.

Research and development produce innovations used in companies and other organisations outside the institution. Regionally engaged HEIs promote the activities and establish structures to support close cooperation with the region. "Service to the community" together with the research, development and education bridge the boundary between the HEI and the region and promote culture community and sustainability. Education and tacit knowledge accumulating through work-based learning in close interaction with working life produce the skills needed and represent "knowledge transfer on legs".

Figure 2. Strategy map of a higher education institution

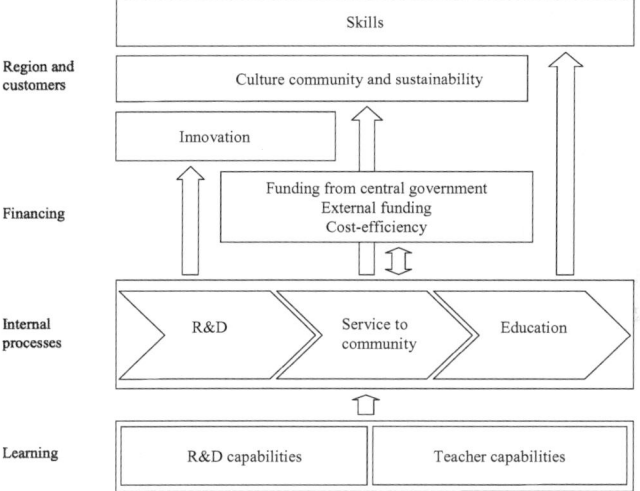

5. Performance evaluation

The philosophies of quality assurance and strategic management using the Balanced Scorecard approach are based on the assumptions: "you can get what you can measure" and "you cannot manage if you cannot measure". The management must be able to define strategic objectives, which are based on the strategic plans of the organisation. The management must also be able to develop the internal processes and structures of the organisation to achieve the strategic objectives. In addition, the management must be able to define measures (indicators) that describe the achievement of strategic objectives.

The objectives in the perspectives of the Balanced Scorecard are balanced between the external measures for the region and customer satisfaction, the objectives of finance that are aligned with the objectives of the internal processes in the budgeting process and the objectives of organisational learning that drive future performance. The objectives are described by the measures, which have target values for the planning period. The advantage of the approach is that it provides information from many perspectives, but tries to reduce information overload describing the objectives and measures which are relevant to implement the strategic plan.

Next the structure of the measures is described using the data available at the national database of the Finnish universities of applied sciences. Following the structure of the quality map the performance evaluation of HEIs should include, among others, following measures:

1. Region and customers
   a) Share of entrepreneurs among graduates
   b) Share of employed among graduates
   c) Share of graduates remaining in the region
   d) Share of theses written for working life
   e) Student satisfaction
   f) Employer satisfaction
   g) Number of applicants per study place
2. Financing
   a) Funding from central government
   b) External funding
   c) Measures of cost efficiency
3. Internal processes
   a) Volume of research and development
   b) Number of publications
   c) Number of degrees awarded
   d) Average duration of study
   e) Average number of credits taken
   f) Student drop-outs rate
   g) Number of outgoing exchange students
   h) Number of incoming exchange students
   i) Number of credits achieved through e-learning
4. Learning
   a) Number of doctorates among the personnel
   b) Number of teachers with teacher training

The measures should be selected so as to describe the achievement of the strategic objectives defined in the strategy map. The best measures indicate the strategic plan so well that it can be inferred by the collection of strategic objectives and measures and the causal relationships among them (Kaplan and Norton, 1996). Educational institutions usually select approximately two dozen measures for their Balanced Scorecards. The measures selected are typically those available in the national database of HEIs.

6. Conclusions

Even though the aim of the quality assurance agencies and ministers of education is not to harmonise the diverse quality assurance systems, this study proposes a step towards a predetermined model but allows flexibility for individual HEIs to build their own quality assurance systems and apply their own procedures for future planning. A common framework is indeed needed, because it increases the objectivity of the external evaluation and helps the HEI to improve its management for improved quality and performance.

The quality and strategy maps have been developed from the basic concepts of quality assurance and strategic management. Both of these management approaches originally developed independently of each other, but they converge at HEIs and many other organisations. The quality and strategy maps presented in this study provide a general conceptual framework to evaluate institutional quality and performance. Both of them can be used independently of each other. Each organisation and evaluator can redefine its own framework following the basic principles of quality assurance and the Balanced Scorecard approach.

The quality map can be used in the quality audits to provide a broad overview of the quality assurance system. It helps the management, personnel and stakeholders of the institution to get the big picture of the quality assurance system. It is also useful to the external evaluators, who have a relatively short time to make their judgements about the quality assurance system of the HEI. The quality map may assume slightly different forms in various kinds of organisations such as the universities of applied sciences and the traditional universities.

The strategy map is a useful tool for describing and evaluating the strategic plan and the performance of the organisation. The strategic objectives are balanced between the external objectives of the environment and customers, the objectives of finance aligned with the activities in the budgeting process, the objectives of internal processes describing the value chain of activities, and the learning objectives that drive future performance. The essence of the strategy is in the activities of an organisation, but all these perspectives are important to ensure the performance of an institution.

Each institution can create its own strategy map. In public sector organisations, the customer receives the service which is the primary objective of these organisations. Therefore it is reasonable to place the recipient at the top of the hierarchy in contrast to private companies, where the financial result is the primary objective. In some public sector organisations, the customer perspective has been divided into societal effects and customer satisfaction. At HEIs, the societal effects essentially describe how the institutions are engaged with the regional development.

References

Berlin Communiqué (2003), "Bologna Process Berlin 2003, Realising the European Higher Education Area", Communiqué of the Conference of Ministers Responsible for Higher Education in Berlin on 19 September 2003.

Davies, B. and Ellison, L. (2003), *The New Strategic Direction and Development of the School*, Routledge Falmer, London.

Deming, W.E. (1986), *Out of the Crisis*, Center for Advanced Engineering Study, Cambridge.

European Association for Quality Assurance in Higher Education (2005), "Standards and guidelines for quality assurance in the European Higher Education Area", available at: http://www.enqa.eu/files/BergenReport210205.pdf (accessed 20 March 2008).

Fidler, B. (2002), *Strategic Management for School Development*, Paul Chapman Publishing, London.

Filippakou, O. and Tapper, T. (2007), "Quality assurance in higher education: thinking beyond the English experience", *Higher Education Policy*, Vol. 20 No. 3, pp. 339-60

Finnish Higher Education Evaluation Council (2008), Audits of quality assurance systems of Finnish higher education institutions, Audit manual for 2008-2011, Finnish Higher Education Evaluation Council 10:2007, available at: http://www.kka.fi/pdf/julkaisut/KKA_1007.pdf (accessed 20 March 2008).

Harvey, L. (2004), Analytic quality glossary, Quality Research International, available at: http://www.qualityresearchinternational.com/glossary/ (accessed 20 March 2008).

Houston, D. (2008), "Rethinking quality and improvement in higher education", *Quality Assurance in Education*, Vol. 16 No. 1, pp. 61-79.

Goddard, J.B. and P. Chatterton (2003), "The response of universities to regional needs", in Boekema, F., Kuypers, E. and Rutten, R. (Eds.), *Economic Geography of Higher Education: Knowledge, Infrastructure and Learning Regions*, London, Routledge, pp. 19-41.

Kaplan, R.S. and Norton, D.P. (1996), *Translating Strategy Into Action, The Balanced Scorecard*, Harvard Business School Press, Boston, MA.

Kaplan, R.S. and Norton, D.P. (2001), *The Strategy-Focused Organization, How Balanced Scorecard Companies Thrive in the New Business Environment*, Harvard Business School Press, Boston, MA.

Kaplan, R.S. and Norton, D.P. (2004), *Strategy Maps, Converting the Intangible Assets into Tangible Outcomes*, Harvard Business School Press, Boston, MA.

Kettunen, J. (2004a), "Bridge building for the future of Finnish polytechnics", *Journal of Higher Education Outreach and Engagement*, Vol. 9 No. 2, pp. 43-57.

Kettunen, J. (2004b), "The strategic evaluation of regional development in higher education", *Assessment & Evaluation in Higher Education*, Vol. 29 No. 3, pp. 357-68.

Kettunen, J. (2005), "Implementation of strategies in continuing education", *The International Journal of Educational Management*, Vol. 19 No. 3, pp. 207-17.

Kettunen, J. (2006a), "Strategies for the cooperation of educational institutions and companies in mechanical engineering", *The International Journal of Educational Management*, Vol. 20 No. 1, pp. 19-28.

Kettunen, J. (2006b), "Strategic planning of regional development in higher education", *Baltic Journal of Management*, Vol. 1 No. 3, pp. 259-69.

Kettunen, J. (2007), "The strategic evaluation of academic libraries", *Library Hi Tech*, Vol. 25 No. 3, pp. 409-21.

Kettunen, J. and Kantola, I. (2005), "Management information system based on the Balanced Scorecard", *Campus-Wide Information Systems*, Vol. 22 No. 5, pp. 263-74.

Maassen, P. and Stensaker, B. (2003), "Interpretations of self-regulation: The changing state-higher education relationship in Europe", in Begg, R. (Ed.), *The Dialogue Between Higher Education Research and Practice*, Dordrecht, Kluwer Academic Publishers, pp. 85-95.

Ministry of Education, Finland (2004), "Quality assurance of higher education", Reports of the Ministry of Education, Finland 2004:6, Helsinki University Press, Helsinki.

Moses, I. (2007), "Institutional autonomy revisited: autonomy justified and accounted", *Higher Education Policy*, Vol. 20 No. 3, pp. 261-74.

Salmi, J. (2007), "Autonomy from the state vs responsiveness to markets", *Higher Education Policy*, Vol. 20 No. 3, pp. 223-42.

OECD (2007), *Higher Education and Regions, Globally Competitive, Locally Engaged*, Organisation for Economic Co-operation and Development. OECD Publishing, Paris.

Steiss, A.W. (2003), *Strategic Management for Public and Nonprofit Organisations*, Marcel Dekker, New York.

Stensaker, B. and Harvey, L. (2006), "Old wine in new bottles? A comparison of public and private accreditation schemes in higher education", *Higher Education Policy*, Vol. 19 No. 1, pp. 65–85.

Tague, N.R. (2004), The quality toolbox, Second Edition, ASQ Quality Press, available at: http://www.asq.org/quality-press/display-item/index.html?item=H1224 (accessed 20 March 2008).

Temponi, C. (2005), "Continuous improvement framework: implications for academia", *Quality Assurance in Education*, Vol. 13 No. 1, pp. 17-36.

III. Bridge Building for the Future of the Finnish Polytechnics

1. Introduction

This chapter presents the process of strategic planning for higher education institutions (HEI) using the Balanced Scorecard approach developed by Kaplan and Norton (1992, 1993). The Balanced Scorecard is an efficient method for the communication and implementation of the strategy. This study extends the Balanced Scorecard to strategic planning and presents how it was successfully used for the network of all the polytechnics in Finland.

The Balanced Scorecard includes a set of measures that give top managers a fast but comprehensive view of the organisation. The perspectives of the Balanced Scorecard include operational measures of customer outcomes. They also include financial measures, internal processes and the organisation's innovation and improvement activities. The Balanced Scorecard has been used across a wide variety of educational organisations (O'Neil et al. 1999)

Strategic management requires understanding of the value creation and causal chains between the objectives of the perspectives. The conception of organisational theory is the basis for the strategic themes, which describe the causal relationships for value creation and reflect the actions that must be taken during the planning horizon to achieve strategic outcomes.

The strategy was planned in 2003 for all the Finnish polytechnics at the meetings of the Rectors' Conference of Finnish Polytechnics. This is a confederation of all the 31 Finnish polytechnics and their owners. It arranges meetings for the rectors and owners of the polytechnics and aims to influence the educational policy in favour of its member organisations. The national strategy provides the outlines for the strategic planning of each polytechnic.

Each HEI can define its own strategic themes consistent with the national strategy. Thus each institution can define its own objectives, measures and performance targets. Then it can implement the strategy using the Balanced Scorecard. Consequently each polytechnic can see how it can contribute to the high-level strategic theme that has been planned jointly between all the polytechnics.

This chapter is organised as follows: Section 2 presents the perspectives of the Balanced Scorecard for use in strategic planning. Section 3 presents the objectives and their causal relationships using a strategy map. The Balanced Scorecard and strategy map provide a general framework for communicating and implementing the strategy, and for understanding the theory of organisation. Section 4 presents the strategic themes and the vision for the future. Finally, the results of the study are summarized and discussed in the concluding section.

2. Perspectives of the Balanced Scorecard

Strategic management is a matter of bridge building, or mapping the route between the perceived present situation and the desired future situation (Wheale, 1991, West-Burnham, 1994). Strategic management involves taking a view of the whole organisation, its place in its environment, its values and culture, its key purpose, its direction and its strategic choice for a better future (Middlewood and Lumby, 1998, Bush and Coleman, 2000, Kettunen, 2002, 2003).

The Balanced Scorecard provides a framework for the implementation of the strategy from four different perspectives: customer, financial, internal processes, and learning and growth. These perspectives have been found necessary, sufficient and robust across a wide variety of organisations (Kaplan and Norton, 1996, 2001).

The results of the study by Lingle and Shieman (1996) show that measurement-managed organisations tend to have better teamwork at the top, better communication throughout the organisation and better self-management at the bottom level. A survey by Frigio and Krumwiede (1999) concluded that performance management systems based on the Balanced Scorecards were significantly more effective compared to other systems.

Customer and financial measures are lagging indicators that report on outcomes. The measures of internal processes describe the organisation's current effectiveness, structure and performance. Learning and growth measures are leading indicators that communicate the drivers of future performance. They are indicators of how to create new value through investments in innovation, technology, employees and customers.

The customer perspective translates an organisation's mission and strategy into specific market- and customer-based objectives. The essence of strategy is not just choosing what to do. It also requires choosing what not to do (Simons, 1995, Treacy and Wiersema, 1995). Institutions that try to be everything to everybody usually end up being nothing to anyone.

The educational institutions should have a clear idea of their desired students. Where do they come from and where do they go? They should have a selected set of outcome measures such as the share of applicants and graduates by region and employment rate. These outcome measures represent the targets for educational institution's marketing, student recruitment, co-operation and employment processes.

The customer perspective enables educational institutions to align their core customer outcome measures to targeted customers. There are generally two sets of objectives for the customer perspective. The first set of objectives includes generic measures, such as customer satisfaction used by virtually all organisations. The second set of objectives represents the segmented performance indicators describing the external impact of HEIs on their local communities.

The financial perspective with traditional financial measures is indicative of past events. The Balanced Scorecard retains traditional financial measures, but expands them to include other perspectives. It complements financial measures of past performance with measures of the present time and measures of the drivers of future performance.

The traditional financial accounting model implicitly incorporates the valuation of an organisation's intangible and intellectual assets. Skilled and motivated employees, effective internal processes, high-quality products and services, and satisfied and loyal customers represent the valuable intangible assets which should result in financial indicators. In many information age organisations these intangible assets and capabilities may be much more important than the financial accounting indicators.

The financial perspective describes the sequence of funding actions that must be taken. It is aligned with the internal process perspective. The objectives of the financial perspectives include the funding of research and development and the funding of education. Funding is a prerequisite for education, but on the other hand efficient processes enable sufficient funding.

The internal processes perspective identifies the critical processes in which the organisation must excel in order to meet the objectives of the strategy. The focus is on monitoring and improving cost, quality and time-based measures of internal processes. Each organisation has a unique set of processes for creating value for customers and producing results. According to Porter (1996) the essence of strategy is in the activities. It is a choice to perform activities differently or to perform different activities than others. The activities are embodied in the value chain, which is described in the internal processes perspective. Consequently strategic themes are connected with the value chain.

An internal-process value chain starts with the innovation process, where the research and development identifies new findings and develops new solutions. The value chain proceeds then to the learning process, where the education disseminates the existing knowledge and services to customers. These processes reflect the traditional mission of HEIs to create and disseminate new knowledge. Educational institutions can choose objectives from themes relating to the efficiency and effectiveness of their main processes.

The learning and growth perspective has strategic objectives, which could include the building of the level of skills and competencies to facilitate the effective internal processes, which are in a key position to reach the objectives in the other perspectives. Expenditures on learning and growth should also be seen as long-term human-resource investments to sustain future development.

When managers are evaluated solely on the short-term financial perspective, they often find it difficult to sustain investments to enhance the capacity of their people. The expenditures on such investments should not be treated as mere period expenses, where cutbacks can be made to produce incremental financial results.

The learning and growth perspective includes the drivers for the objectives and outcomes in the other perspectives. It includes the capabilities of the personnel to successfully fulfil the actions in the internal processes perspective. The operative actions regarding these capabilities can be classified into recruitment and internal training. The decisions regarding these actions should be weighed against the strategic plan of the organisation.

3. Objectives and their causal relationships

A survey was made in February 2003 of the most important objectives of the Finnish polytechnics. Altogether 29 rectors of Finnish polytechnics filled in the form and responded to the questions at the general meeting of the rectors' conference. The purpose of the survey was to identify the most important objectives for the strategic plan of the Finnish polytechnics.

Table 1 presents the results of the survey. Regional development and employer and student satisfaction are the most important objectives in the customer perspective. The funding of research and development, and the funding of education by central government are the most important objectives in the financial perspective. Research and development and education can be selected from the internal processes perspective for closer analysis. Finally, capabilities for research and development, and personnel development can be selected from the learning and growth perspective.

The results of the survey are reasonable and consistent, because research and development and education have the highest scores in the financial, internal processes, and learning and growth perspectives. They are the most important activities, which create value for customers and can be selected for the basis of the strategic plan.

Table 1. Perceptions of rectors of the development of the Finnish polytechnics

	Mean on a scale 1-5
Customer perspective	
• Regional development	4.3
• Employer satisfaction	4.4
• Student satisfaction	4.4
• Satisfaction of the owners of polytechnics	4.0
Financial perspective	
• External funding	3.9
• Funding of R&D	4.4
• Funding of education by central government	4.7
• Funding of investments	4.3
Internal processes perspective	
• R&D	4.5
• Support activities	3.3
• Education	4.8
Learning and growth perspective	
• R&D	4.3
• Environmental scanning and customer knowledge	4.1
• Quality and assessment	3.8
• Personnel development	4.6

The strategy is a set of hypotheses about cause and effect. The Balanced Scorecard provides a general framework for understanding the causal chains. The perspectives, objectives and measures, and the linkages among them describe the organisational theory (cf. Drucker, 1994). The definition of these linkages may be based on research, experience or hypotheses.

The strategic plan should make the hypotheses among objectives in the various perspectives explicit so that they can be managed and validated. The linkages of the scorecard should incorporate a set of cause-and-effect relationships among the objectives and describe the strategy. They should incorporate mixtures of performance drivers and outcome measures.

The multiple measures should describe the internal processes describing the chain of value creation and consist of a linked series of objectives which are consistent and mutually reinforcing. The value chain becomes simpler to understand and manage when it is viewed as a sequential process moving from left to right on the diagram.

The strategy maps by Kaplan and Norton (2001) provide a logical way to communicate the organisation's desired outcomes and how these outcomes can be achieved. The linkages in strategy maps describe the cause-and-effect relationships between the perspectives and for value creation over the planning horizon.

The objectives in the customer perspective are desired outcomes, but the strategy map does not explain in detail how to achieve them. The internal processes define the activities needed to create the desired value proposition for customers. The financial perspective defines the funding needed to enable the internal processes. The learning and growth perspective develops the ability to execute internal processes. It is based on the skills and knowledge of employees and the technology they use.

Figure 1 presents the strategy map of the Finnish polytechnics describing the causal chains between the objectives. The objectives are based on the survey conducted on the rectors of polytechnics. The linkages between the perspectives and objectives are based on the discussion between the rectors and representatives of the owners of the polytechnics.

The vertical cause-and-effect relationships describe the chain of value creation between the drivers that will lead to the strategic and desired objectives. Examining the linkages between the perspectives and objectives leads to the conclusion that an increase in the target measure in the customer perspective would result from the activities in the internal processes perspective, which requires funding and capabilities for performing the necessary activities.

The customer perspective contains two objectives namely employer and student satisfaction and regional development. These objectives can be achieved by the activities of the research and development and education described in the internal processes perspective.

The financial perspective includes two objectives namely the funding of research and development and the funding of education by central government. The funding of research and development includes internal funding from central government and external funding from other sources. The education is funded by central government, but it receives some minor funding through commercial services.

The internal processes perspective includes a description of the horizontal sequential processes including innovation and learning processes, which form the conventional causal chain of value creation in higher education. The objectives in the financial, and learning and growth perspectives have to be achieved in order to ensure efficient internal processes, which result in the desired outcomes in regional development and customer satisfaction. The objectives of the internal processes perspective include the efficiency of research and development and education.

The objectives in the learning and growth perspective include the capabilities for research and development and personnel development. HEIs must have capabilities for research and development to generate new knowledge in the internal processes. Personnel development is necessary to develop education and achieve high-quality learning.

4. Strategic themes and the vision for the future

Strategic themes

The strategic themes reflect what management believes must be done to succeed and to achieve strategic outcomes. The strategic themes are strategic hypotheses containing their own set of cause-and-effect relationships. Each of the internal processes is connected to the strategic themes.

Figure 1. Strategy map of Finnish polytechnics

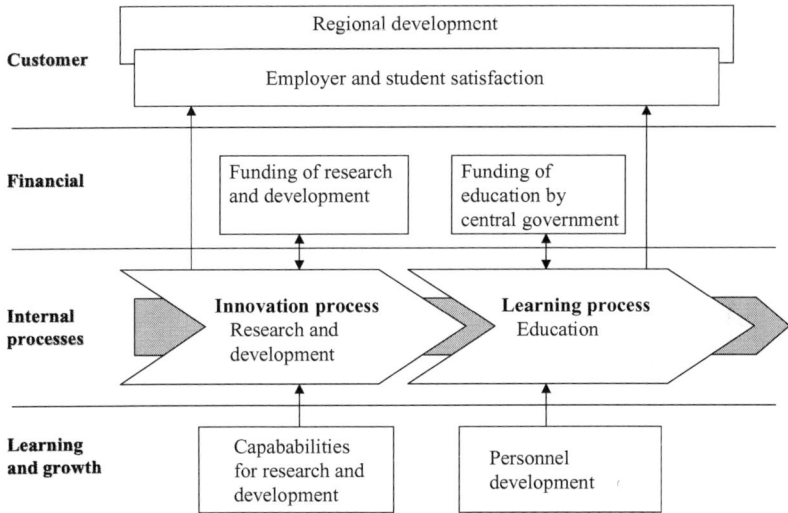

In March 2003 the rectors of the polytechnics and the representatives of the owners began the planning of the strategy using the perspectives of the Balanced Scorecard. Altogether 53 individuals participated in the process, which was based on the preliminary survey conducted earlier. The most important objectives of the survey were selected for detailed planning.

When the most important objectives were well understood, the purpose was to define ways to achieve these goals. The participants in the strategy process were divided into four groups selected according to the perspectives. The participants tried to see how the particular measures, targets and strategic initiatives contribute to achieving the objectives.

Tables 2-5 present the strategic themes and their detailed contents based on the results of the working groups. The strategic themes describe postgraduate education, quality of education, research and development, and regional development. They do not include any financial themes, because the financial result is not the main purpose of public educational organisations. An advantage of the Balanced Scorecard is that each strategic theme is balanced describing the policy and objectives in each perspective.

The polytechnics defined their strategy around the main strategic theme and four strategic themes as follows:

Theory and practice in a balanced mixture
* *Permanent postgraduate degrees will be established after the experimental period*
* *Polytechnics will improve the quality of education*
* *Research and development will serve education*
* *Research and development and education will develop the region*

The scorecard should be the mechanism by which the senior executives present their organisation's strategies to their boards of directors and stakeholders. Senior executives become committed to and accountable for achieving the organisational vision by establishing short and long-term targets and directing strategic initiatives and resources toward achieving them.

The preliminary strategy of the Finnish polytechnics was first presented in May 2003 to a wide audience including staff from polytechnics and other organisations in the General Meeting of Finnish Polytechnics. The representatives from the most important stakeholders made valuable and positive comments.

Table 2. Permanent postgraduate degrees will be established after the experimental period

Customer	*Employer and student satisfaction:* • Employers will be satisfied with the development projects in postgraduate education • Students will be satisfied with the emerging opportunities for postgraduate education and capabilities for R&D
Financial	*Funding by central government:* • Funding for the postgraduate degrees will be arranged
Internal processes	*Learning process:* • Postgraduate degrees will be established as a part of the Bologna Process • The dual system of universities and polytechnics will remain and be strengthened • Education will use the results of the expanding R&D
Learning and growth	*Personnel development:* • The polytechnics will increase the number of licentiates and doctorates taken • The capabilities for R&D will be increased in order to improve education • Postgraduate degrees from polytechnics will constitute competence for lecturerships

Table 3. Polytechnics will improve the quality of education

Customer	*Employer and student satisfaction:* • Education will have external impact especially on small and medium sized enterprises • Employers will obtain skilled labour that meet their needs • Students will be satisfied with good employment opportunities
Financial	*Funding by central government:* • The incentive effects will be implemented in the new funding system
Internal processes	*Learning process:* • Learning processes will be made more efficient • Education will use the results of the expanding R&D
Learning and growth	*Personnel development:* • The capabilities of personnel for the co-operation with companies and other organisations will be improved

Table 4. Research and development will serve education

Customer	*Employer and student satisfaction:* • R&D will meet the needs of the local economy • The number of R&D projects having regional impact will be large • R&D will serve education
Financial	*Funding of R&D:* • The basic funding for R&D will be organized • External funding based on stipulated systems will be increased • Publication will be organised effectively and the number of publications will be increased
Internal processes	*Innovation process:* • R&D will be organized effectively in each polytechnic • R&D environments will be developed with working life • Publishing will be developed and the number of publications will be increased
Learning and growth	*Capabilities for R&D:* • The competitive advantage of polytechnics will be increased in order to increase the funding for R&D • The number of R&D programmes will be increased and networks will be strengthened

Table 5. Research and development and education will develop the region

	R&D:	*Education:*
Customer	*Regional development:* • R&D will support the regional development in the innovation system • Municipal R&D will serve the local economy	*Regional development:* • Students will have good employment opportunities in the region • Education will meet the needs of the region
Financial	*Funding of R&D:* • Regional funding of the innovation system of SMEs will be arranged • Regional funding of R&D will be arranged • External funding will be arranged to transform the innovations into action	*Funding of education:* • Theses will be done for companies and other organisations • Long-term contracts will be made to facilitate co-operation
Internal processes	*Innovation process:* • The number of joint R&D projects with working life will be increased • R&D will focus on the strengths of polytechnics	*Learning process:* • Co-operation with SMEs and universities will be increased • Entrepreneurship will be promoted by incubators
Learning and growth	*Capabilities for R&D:* • Capabilities for project work will be enhanced • Polytechnic will increase their knowledge about the activities and needs of the municipalities	*Personnel development:* • Environmental scanning will be done and customer needs will be studied

The vision for the future

The next phase of the process was to plan the vision for the year 2010. In June 2003 the rectors were divided into four groups according to the strategic themes. The purpose was to plan details for each theme using the perspectives of the Balanced Scorecard. The themes of the vision describe the state of the strategic themes in 2010. The themes of the vision can be written as follows:

Advanced knowledge for working life
• *Postgraduate education will be based on the needs of regions and serve working life*
• *New methods will be used in high-quality education*
• *Education will be based on the results of research and development*
• *Research and development, education and regional development will support closely each other*

Table 6 presents the description of the vision by strategic theme. Each theme has been described from the perspectives of the Balanced Scorecard in order to describe the vision in a balanced way. The procedure ensures that the details of the vision are consistent with the strategic themes defined earlier.

At the end of 2003 the board of the Rectors' Conference of Finnish Polytechnics put the final touches to the strategic plan including the vision for the future. The plan was finally accepted at the General Meeting of the Rectors' Conference of Finnish Polytechnics in March 2004.

Table 6. The vision of Finnish polytechnics by strategic themes

Postgraduate education: Postgraduate education will be based on the needs of regions and serve working life
• The strengths of postgraduate education will be selected to meet the needs of the regions
• Postgraduate education will be funded by the sources targeted at adult education
• Efficient postgraduate education will be based on the dual model of universities and polytechnics
• R&D will serve the postgraduate education, which will constitute competence for the lecturerships

Quality of education: New methods are used in high-quality education
• Education will meet the needs of regional working life
• The process of learning will be efficient and cost-effective
• New methods will be used in education based on the R&D
• 25 % of the resources will be used in R&D

R&D: Education will be based on the results of R&D
• Polytechnics will be well-known and strong actors in regional R&D
• R&D will have permanent funding
• R&D will be firmly linked to education and regional development
• R&D will be of high quality and its job structure will be well-developed

Regional development: R&D, education and regional development will closely support each other
• Polytechnics will play a leading role in the development of municipalities and regions
• Funding for regional development will be achieved
• Polytechnics will be leading actors in interdisciplinary projects
• The knowledge of the polytechnics in regional development will be advanced

5. Conclusions

The study extended the Balanced Scorecard from the communication and implementation of the strategy to the planning of the strategy. An advantage of the approach is that the strategic plan describes the activities needed in a balanced way, taking into account all the necessary perspectives of the plan. The balanced strategic plan also facilitates the communication and successful implementation of the strategy.

The strategy of Finnish polytechnics represents the collective wisdom of rectors, owners and other stakeholders of polytechnics. Without actively engaging these partners in the process of strategic planning, a successful outcome is unlikely. In a successful case the strategy drives change and becomes an integral part of the management process of the Rectors' Conference of Finnish Polytechnics.

The strategy of the Finnish polytechnics describes the objectives and measures needed to reach these goals. It is a strategy that has been formulated for the network of polytechnics, which is responsible for the implementation of the strategy. Once the strategy has been articulated for the Finnish polytechnics, each polytechnic can develop its strategy and scorecard describing how its internal processes will deliver the output to implement the general strategy.

The high-level national strategy will need updating when the environment of HEIs changes or when the main objectives of the strategic themes have been achieved. In addition, the change in educational policy may be great enough to change the strategy. The national strategy can be revised updating the high-level strategic themes and objectives. The updating the strategies of HEIs involves changes in the strategic themes, objectives, measures and target values.

References

Bush, T. and M. Coleman (2000), Leadership and Strategic Management in Education, London: Paul Chapman Publishing.

Drucker, P. (1994), The Theory of Business, Harvard Business Review, September-October, 95-104.

Frigio, M.L. and K. Krumwiede (1999), Balanced Scorecard: A Rising Trend in Strategic Performance Measurement, Journal of Strategic Performance Measurement, February-March, 42-48.

Kaplan, R. and D. Norton (1992), The Balanced Scorecard: Measures that Drive Performance, Harvard Business Review, January-February, 71-79.

Kaplan, R. and D. Norton (1993), Putting the Balanced Scorecard to Work, Harvard Business Review, September-October, 134-147.

Kaplan, R. and D. Norton (1996), The Balanced Scorecard, Boston, Massachusetts: Harvard Business School Press.

Kaplan, R. and D. Norton (2001), The Strategy-Focused Organization, Boston, Massachusetts: Harvard Business School Press.

Kettunen, J. (2002), Competitive Strategies in Higher Education, Journal of Institutional Research 11, 38-47.

Kettunen, J. (2003), Strategic Evaluation of Institutions by Students in Higher Education, Perspectives: Policy and Practice in Higher Education 7, 14-18.

Lingle, J.H. and W.A. Shieman (1996), From Balanced Scorecards to Strategic Gauges: Is Measurement Worth It? Management Review, March, 56-62.

Middlewood, D. and J. Lumby (1998), Strategic Management in Schools and Colleges, London: Paul Chapman Publishing Ltd.

O'Neil, H.F.Jr., E.M. Besimon, M.A. Diamond and M.R. Moore (1999), Designing and Implementing an Academic Scorecard, Change 31, 32-40.

Porter, M. (1996), What is Strategy? Harvard Business Review, November-December, 61-78.

Simons, R. (1995), Levers of Control: How Managers Use Innovative Control Systems to Drive Strategic Renewal, Boston: Harvard Business School Press, 47-55, 156.

Treacy M. and F. Wiersema (1995), The Discipline of Market Leaders: Choose Your Customers, Narrow Your Focus, Dominate Your Market, Reading, MA: Addison-Wesley.

West-Burnham, J. (1994), Strategy, Policy and Planning, In T. Bush and J. West-Burnham (eds.), The Principles of Educational Management, Harlow, Longman.

Wheale, J. (1991), Generating Income for Educational Institutions: A Business Planning Approach, London: Kogan Page.

IV. The Strategic Evaluation of Academic Libraries

1. Introduction

Strategic planning has an important role in academic libraries (Adeyoyin, 2005, Huotari and Iivonen, 2005, Decker and Höppner, 2006). The libraries have developed networked cooperation to develop their activities. The cooperation has led to the planning of network strategic plans to guide the future cooperation of the network. The network strategy is different from the strategy of a single organisation, because there is no single organisation which owns the strategy or is responsible for implementing and evaluating it. The network strategy aims to achieve strategic objectives that cannot be achieved by any single library alone.

A high degree of autonomy and professional discretion are characteristics of universities (O'Neil et al., 1999). The autonomy of universities has increased and self-management has become increasingly important. These characteristics, on the other hand, emphasise the accountability of the universities. They are increasingly accountable for results and face growing expectations, which underline the need for a rational framework to evaluate institutional strategic plans and performance. This study analyses the evaluation of the strategic plans and performance of academic libraries.

Each strategic plan has particular merits that are related to the external environment, internal processes and structures, financial resources and human capabilities. Strategic evaluation is used to judge these merits and the implementation of the strategy. The evaluation of strategic plans requires a framework and sensible judgements on different strategic objectives weighed against each other. The various strategic objectives should be aligned with each other in a balanced way so that the strategic management is able to build bridges between the perceived present situation and the desired future position described by the vision (Bush and Coleman, 2000, Fidler, 2002, Johnson and Scholes, 2002).

A rational framework to evaluate strategic plans can be found among the tools of strategic planning. The Balanced Scorecard developed by Kaplan and Norton (1996, 2001) was developed as a framework to communicate and implement strategic plans. It has turned out that the Balanced Scorecard approach can also be used to plan strategies (Kettunen, 2004a, b). It is also important to find a rational framework to evaluate the strategic plans and performance. Otherwise the evaluation is based on subjective judgements of different individuals.

The Balanced Scorecard approach measures the implementation of the strategic plan across customers, finance, internal processes and learning. The measures are balanced between the external measures for customers, the measures of finance, the measures of internal processes, and the learning measures that drive future performance. The Balanced Scorecard provides information from many perspectives in a balanced combination. Therefore the approach is also ideal for the evaluation of strategic plans even though the Balanced Scorecard approach has not been used in the planning of the strategies.

The purpose of this chapter is to present a general approach to the evaluation of strategic plans and their implementation. The approach is applied to describe and communicate the strategic plans of the consortium of the digital libraries of 29 Finnish universities of applied sciences and their strategic plan for the Web service. The purpose of the consortium is to promote cooperation between the libraries especially in their electronic services. This is an example of fruitful cooperation between institutions.

The concept of the strategy map developed by Kaplan and Norton (2001, 2004) is used to describe and communicate the network strategies of the libraries. The efficient communication of strategic objectives is important especially in a network strategy which is planned and implemented by many libraries. The diverse backgrounds of libraries underline the need for enhanced communication. The strategy map helps the personnel of the libraries to create a shared understanding about the strategic objectives.

This chapter is organised as follows: The following section first introduces the main characteristics of the consortium of the libraries of the Finnish universities of applied sciences and their shared strategic plans. Next, the perspectives of the Balanced Scorecard approach are discussed and the strategy map of the consortium of libraries is presented. Thereafter, the strategic plans of the consortium are evaluated using the different perspectives of the Balanced Scorecard. Finally, the results of the study are summarized and discussed in the concluding section.

2. Strategic planning of the consortium of academic libraries

The strategic plan of the consortium

The consortium of the libraries of the Finnish universities of applied sciences was founded in 2001 to coordinate cooperation between the respective libraries of the institutions (AMKIT Consortium, 2007). Higher education in Finland is divided into 20 traditional research-oriented universities and 29 profession-oriented universities of applied sciences. Even though higher education is segmented in two sectors, their libraries cooperate actively with each other. Libraries are excellent examples where the advantages of networking emerge (Gallimore, 1999, Poll, 2001, Jin, 2004).

The libraries of the universities of applied sciences have nearly 500 workers located in 80 towns and 200 places. The remotely located branches of the libraries reflect the relatively short history of the universities of applied sciences in Finland. These institutions were established at the beginning of the 1990s by separating parts from the vocational institutions. The first institutions were in the field of technology and transport, which is why at the beginning of their history the institutions were called polytechnics until the end of 2005.

The consortium of libraries is a useful network, which cooperates and exchanges information and obtains financial benefits from its institutions and the Ministry of Education. The consortium prepared a joint strategy for the planning period 2004-2007. The joint strategy is clearly linked to the education policy, but on the other hand it is included in the strategic planning of their home institutions. Much of the success of the libraries and the universities of applied sciences lies in how the network strategies can be aligned with the strategies of the institutions.

The Finnish universities of applied sciences have planned an overall network strategy for the institutions (Kettunen, 2004b). The network strategy provides the insight and direction to guide the strategic planning of each university of applied sciences. Naturally each autonomous institution is responsible for making its own strategic plans. Similarly the network strategy of libraries provides outlines for the future plans of each library. Each library assumes the responsibility to prepare its own strategic plan, define strategic themes and implement them. The action plan describes in detail how the library will implement its strategic plans.

Large organisations typically formulate and communicate their strategic plans using approximately two dozen measures, but the administrative units may use a smaller amount of indicators (Kettunen, 2005). The number of strategic measures depends on how many measures are needed to describe and communicate the strategic plan and avoid sub-optimisation along any single measures. Typically, the partial strategies of the overall strategy are focused on the specific function of the institution such as internationalisation, entrepreneurship or educational development. These partial strategies are not necessarily described by their own sets of measures, but rather are implemented using action plans or development projects.

The strategic themes describe what management believes must be done to succeed and to achieve the desired strategic outcomes. The consortium of libraries has defined general strategic themes to describe the development work for the better future. The strategic themes can be written as follows:
- *The cooperation of libraries is systematic and nationwide.*
- *Libraries cooperate with the consortium of libraries and the institution.*
According to these strategic themes the success of libraries is found within the consortium of libraries and on the other hand in the ability to serve the education institutions.

A clearly articulated vision describes the direction and future of an organisation and helps its administrative units and individuals to understand their roles in supporting the organisation (Fidler, 2002, Kettunen, 2003, Davies and Ellison, 2003). The strategic plan describes the dynamic actions needed for the organisation to change from the present situation to the desired future position described by the vision. The strategy evolves over time and follows the core values and organisational culture and adapts to the changing environment. The strategy arises from the strategic choices and how the activities are performed.

The consortium of libraries has defined its vision in the future as follows:
- *The library is the dynamic interface between education and research.*
- *The library is an efficient and high-quality service point, a partner and developer in the library network, and a notable regional, national and international trend-setter for its subject areas.*
The vision emphasises libraries' desire to be an active and dynamic partner with their home institutions and the surrounding environment. The vision clearly reflects institutions' outreach and engagement activities.

The implementation of the strategic plan relies heavily on the strategic initiatives to implement the plan. The consortium has had numerous cooperation projects including the acquisition and implementation of the Endeavor's Voyager information system, the library portal project, the acquisition of electronic journals, quality management, and the education of information skills and virtual learning environments. The Voyager Library Automation System is also used at the traditional Finnish universities and universities in other countries (Guy, 2000, Pace, 2004, Breeding, 2006).

The strategic plan of digital libraries

Digital technology provides many opportunities and challenges for libraries (Sharma and Wishwanathan, 2001, Frumkin, 2004, Liu, 2004). A specific joint network strategy was planned for the digital libraries to promote their Web service and supplement the overall network strategy. The strategy process was completed and the network strategy was updated in 2006 replacing the earlier strategy approved in 2003. The strategy for digital libraries describes in detail the more general network strategy of the consortium of libraries.

The strategic plan of digital libraries includes four objectives:
* content
* tools
* cooperation
* knowledge

The objective of the plan is to achieve high-quality content and information technology tools of the Web service which effectively support the core processes of the institution. Quality assurance has an important role as in many other libraries (Tam, 2000, Nagata et al., 2004, Rowley, 2005). Education and applied research and development are the core processes of the institution. In order to be effective and high-quality, widespread cooperation with the institution is required. Wide-ranging knowledge is also needed to establish the Web service.

3. The Balanced Scorecard approach

Perspectives

The Balanced Scorecard has been developed to provide a framework for the communication and implementation of the strategy. The approach translates the strategic plan into objectives and measures and balances them into four different perspectives. The system of objectives and measures should indicate the strategic plan through a sequence of relationships between the performance drivers (leading indicators) and outcome objectives (lagging indicators).

The perspectives of the Balanced Scorecard are the following:
1. Customer. The customer perspective includes strategic objectives that are outcomes of past efforts and reports on the outcomes achieved to external stakeholders.
2. Finance. The objectives of the financial perspective are prerequisites for the internal processes and aligned with the activities in the budgeting process.
3. Internal processes. The objectives of the internal processes describe the present performance of the organisation.
4. Learning. The objectives of the learning perspective are drivers for future performance and describe how to create value through investments in innovation, technology and employees.

These perspectives have been found to be necessary and sufficient in a wide variety of organisations.

The objectives are derived from the strategic plan. Therefore the performance of the managers responsible and their organisational units can be directly linked to the strategy. The achievement of the objectives can be ensured by various ways. Some organisations use indicators where target values have been set for the planning period. Other organisations use strategic initiatives which typically develop the internal processes and structures and create value for customers. In addition, development programmes, action plans and workload plans can be used to implement the strategy.

It is argued in this study that it is reasonable to apply the perspectives of the Balanced Scorecard in the evaluation of strategies, because the approach is a safeguard that the strategy can be described and implemented in a balanced manner. The common framework for describing and evaluating the strategy is a prerequisite for successful evaluation. The strategic plan must be understood before it can be communicated and evaluated in a reasonable way. Without a proper framework, the evaluation is based on the personal experiences and belief about the future plans of an organisation.

The customer perspective may need to be rethought for libraries operating within education institutions. Such libraries serve the students and personnel of the institutions and the public at large who benefit from the services of the libraries. On the other hand, the library is part of the institution and takes responsibility, at least in part, for achieving the institution's strategic objectives. Therefore the customer perspective has been placed at the top of the hierarchy.

A strategy map

The network strategy of libraries is analysed in this study using the causal chains of value creation between the perspectives in the strategy map. Kaplan and Norton (2001, 2004) developed the strategy maps to illustrate the written strategy in a graphic form. The strategy map makes explicit the strategic plans by describing a chain of cause-and-effect relationships between the driving forces and the desired strategic outcomes. The strategy map describes the process for transforming intangible assets and financial resources into tangible customer outcomes. The best strategy maps indicate the strategy so well that the strategy can be inferred from the collection of objectives and causal relationships among them.

Figure 1 describes the strategy map of the consortium of libraries. The description of the strategy map can be started in a top-down fashion defining the strategic objectives in the customer perspective. The description can be started by asking, "What does the strategic plan of libraries provide for their customers?" The general strategic objective of the consortium is to support the institutions enabling the high quality of education and research. Another objective is the high-quality content and tools of the Web service which support the education and research.

Another question in the financial perspective is, "What is the funding of the implementation of strategic plans and are there any clearly articulated strategic objectives? The objectives of the financial perspective include the funding from the Ministry of Education and the cost-efficiency. The Ministry of Education has provided additional funding for the development of libraries and promotion of the cooperation among the institutions. Cost-efficiency is an objective which is directly linked to cooperation between libraries.

Then regarding the core of the strategy a question can be asked, "What has to be done in the internal processes and structures and what are the strategic objectives? The objectives of this perspective are the cooperation with the consortium of libraries and the home institution. These aims increase the efficiency of the internal processes and structures of the libraries. The achievements of these objectives support the institution to achieve its strategic objectives.

The last question is, "What learning is required in the libraries?" The objective of the learning perspective is to increase the knowledge and expertise of the personnel. The capabilities of the library personnel are the driving forces to achieve the objectives in the internal processes and finally in the customer perspective. The strategic awareness of libraries is also an objective and a driver for future performance. The strategic awareness is a prerequisite for the cooperation and increased performance.

The libraries adapt their financial resources, internal processes and knowledge to the changing environment. As the environment changes and learning takes place the libraries periodically update their strategic plans. The budgets, action plans and the targets of the measures are updated annually in the network and institutions. If there are no exact and direct measures indicating the strategic objectives, the gaps can be filled by the descriptions written in the action plan. Things do not just happen, they must be carefully planned.

The strategy map provides a simple tool for illustrating and evaluating the strategic plans. The evaluation of the strategic plans using the strategy map leads to the conclusion that the written strategy provides a balanced mix of strategic objectives. There are reasonable objectives in all the perspectives. Another remark is that reasonable causal linkages can be drawn between the objectives. If the strategy is understood, it can be executed.

The network strategies can be shared to achieve synergy across autonomous organisations. Strategic themes, strategy maps and action plans can be used to achieve commitment to a common network strategy, but it is not necessary to define the measures and performance targets for the network strategy. Each institution and library can define its own strategic themes, objectives, measures and performance targets and implement them using the Balanced Scorecard. Consequently, each library can see how it contributes to the high-level strategic plan.

Figure 1. The strategy map of the consortium of libraries

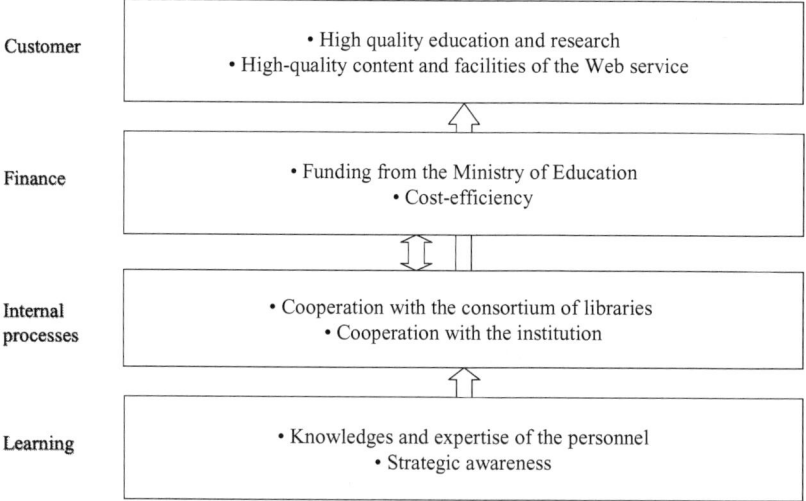

4. Evaluation of strategic plans

Customer perspective

The customer perspective includes the desired outcomes of the activities. It includes the final strategic objectives, which are results of the objectives achieved in the internal processes perspectives. The customer perspective enhances the value created for the customers, because value creation is the purpose of any service unit of an organisation. When the strategic plan is written for an administrative subunit, the customer perspective can be interpreted as implicitly including the strategic objectives of the whole organisation.

The strategic objectives of the customer perspective support the high quality of education and applied research and development. The high-quality content and tools of the Web service clearly also support the objectives of the institutions. These objectives are likely to be achieved by combining resources between the libraries but are unlikely to be realized if each institution operates in isolation. The libraries are essential administrative units of the institutions and support the strategic objectives of the institutions. Some of the objectives can be supported directly, others indirectly.

The action plan should identify the strategic initiatives, timetables and the units and individuals responsible for the implementation of the strategic plan. The action plan should drill the strategic plan down into one or more action plans and include these in the operating budget. The monitoring of these detailed operational plans will then become part of the periodic review process of management. The action plan of the libraries does not include elements which clearly describe the values created for customers.

The evaluation of the customer perspective leads to the conclusion that strategic objectives describe the desired outcome rather briefly. The values created for the students, personnel and other users of the libraries have not been described in detail in the strategic or action plans. The customer-orientation of the future planning would require more detailed explanation how the users can benefit from the services provided by libraries.

Financial perspective

There must be a strong linkage between the financial objectives and internal processes. Funding is a prerequisite for the internal processes, but on the other hand cost-efficiency is required in the internal processes. The financial perspective can emphasise the increase of financial resources to favour better service, but it can also highlight the economical production of services. In public sector organisations, the financial resources are typically limited. These organisations seek efficient ways to produce high quality output given the limited financial resources.

The libraries are primarily funded by the institutions. They also obtain some external income from customers and development projects. These matters have been taken into account only in the budgets of the libraries. The additional funding provided by the Ministry of Education has maintained sufficient coherence of the libraries and ensured that the objectives of network cooperation can be achieved. The utilization of expensive resources is particularly emphasised.

Cost-efficiency can be achieved by investing in physical and intellectual assets across the libraries of institutions. The objective of cost-efficiency is achieved by increasing cooperation between the libraries and taking advantage of the economy of scale across investments. The libraries can increase the leverage from the infrastructure investments by sharing them across multiple institutions. The strategic plan emphasises shared tools and data networks as a means to utilise limited resources in a cost-efficient manner. The strategic plan of libraries also includes joint Web service and development projects.

The action plan of the consortium of libraries includes the purchase of information technology tools with the help of the information technology consortium of the universities of applied sciences. The libraries provide the Web service through various portals including the portal of universities, regional portals and the portal of the Finnish Virtual University of Applied Sciences. The libraries follow how the new tools develop and are prepared to put them to good use.

An important element of the action plan is also that the consortium annually negotiates about the licences for e-resources. They are jointly purchased from Finnish Electronic Library (FinELib) or other sources for the libraries according to the principles described in the portal of the consortium. The libraries also provide the customers with the contents of electronic learning objectives produced by the other universities of applied sciences. The consortium negotiates with the content producers and publishers about the development of e-material appropriate for their respective institutions.

The evaluation of the financial perspective leads to the conclusion that the objectives of the financial perspective are reasonable even though they are limited. The external funding for the research and development does not exist in the plans. The funding from the institutions is also taken for granted. These objectives have remained implicit in the strategic planning, but they have been taken into account in the budgeting process of the institutions.

Internal processes perspective

The strategic plans concentrate mainly on the internal processes. This is reasonable, because the essence of strategy is in the activities. The strategy is not only what the organisation intends to do, but also what it decides not to do (Porter, 1996). The focus of each institution should be based on its strengths, which are the basis for the division of labour and avoiding overlapping activities. This is especially relevant to the education institutions operating in the same district of the city. The cooperation between otherwise independent libraries exemplifies their synergies as the fundamental characteristic of the operation.

The purpose of the network is to identify how the activities of separate education institutions can be combined to create synergies among their libraries. The similar internal processes of the education institutions and libraries favour cooperation. The libraries have articulated the rationale for having relatively close cooperation with each other rather than having each library operating as an independent entity with its self-governing activities. It was fairly straightforward to commit to joint objectives, because the Ministry of Education provided financial support to develop library systems.

According to the action plan, the Web service of libraries provides high-quality collections which can be utilised using the Web. The close cooperation of libraries is essential to construct and maintain the Web services. With the help of the consortium, each library can supplement its collections from FinELib or other acquisition consortia. In addition, the libraries provide the publications of the universities of applied sciences using the Web.

The software, equipment and other tools support the efficient Web service. The libraries provide portals for the students and personnel to acquire information and software of digital libraries. The electronic tools of the library are connected with the institution's other information systems such as the student and study registers and virtual learning environment. The Web service also provides interactive tools such as the real-time network information service.

The libraries participate and establish multidisciplinary and cooperative projects to develop Web services. They make sure that the results of cooperative projects are implemented and utilised after the project is over. The Voyager cooperation will continue. The facility group of the consortium solves problems and establishes a joint catalogue. The technology group of the consortium supports and supervises the development of metadata banks. The libraries are looking for possibilities for promoting the multidisciplinary cooperation in their institutions. The virtual information specialists are seeking ways how the library can support the e-learning of the degree programmes.

The evaluation of the internal processes perspective reveals the main function of the network. According to the action plan, the consortium of libraries will participate actively in the local, national and international networks to better serve the institution. The managers of the consortium believe that the joint investments in the electronic collections and tools will create value for institutions that cannot be otherwise achieved in a cost-efficient manner. It can be concluded that the objectives of the internal processes are well planned and reasonable.

The learning perspective

The learning perspective emphasises investments in human capital. The performance drivers of this perspective should communicate the capabilities necessary to achieve the objectives in the internal processes perspective and finally in the customer perspective. The performance drivers should also provide an early indication about whether the strategy can be successfully implemented.

The objective of the learning perspective is to develop knowledge and expertise among the personnel of the libraries. The investment in human capital is planned to facilitate the cooperation of libraries. Workshops and seminars are typical examples of creating and disseminating knowledge which helps the personnel of the libraries. The strategy process of libraries has also been a joint learning process, where the libraries have documented modes of cooperation and developed new ones.

The strategic plan of digital libraries also emphasises the knowledge of the personnel. The employees should be aware of the electronic collections and be skilled in using them. The libraries also provide counselling and guidance to their customers in the Web. The libraries develop the pedagogical knowledge of their workers, who follow the new opportunities in their field of expertise. The information seeking and management skills promote the aims of information literacy. The concept of information literacy refers to the competence of acquiring, assessing and utilising information and knowledge (Bawden, 2001, Lloyd, 2003, Owusu-Ansah, 2003).

The action plan includes training to promote the skills needed in the Web service. The pedagogical group of the consortium plans and provides training for information literacy. The e-material group of the consortium takes responsibility for arranging workshops and seminars concerning the e-collections. The topics include copyrights, licences, content and e-collections in library education. Training is also provided on metadata for the teachers of the Web service and information specialists. The libraries arrange training in information literacy for students, teachers and personnel in their own institutions. The library personnel is also encouraged to participate in content production and pedagogical training.

The evaluation of the learning perspective leads to the conclusion that the plan provides ample elements for development and increased cooperation. The cooperation is supported by the objectives emphasising knowledge and expertise defined in the learning perspective. It is evident that the joint training for the library personnel is aligned with the development of cooperation and is inclined to increase the cooperation between the libraries. The causal relationships between the objectives have not been explained in detail in the strategic plan, but the implicit cause-and-effect relationships are evident.

5. Conclusions

The strategic plans have been made for the consortium of libraries, because no single library has complete control over all the aspects that are necessary to achieve the desired objectives and service quality. The strategic themes, objectives and outlines of the action plans were first formulated for the network. Then each library was able to define its own strategic themes, objectives and action plans to contribute the network strategy and the overall strategy of the institution.

The network strategic plans of libraries are relatively well balanced including reasonable strategic objectives in the perspectives of the Balanced Scorecard. The consortium and individual libraries have aligned their financial and human resources with the internal processes to achieve the desired objectives in the customer perspective. It can also be concluded that the majority of the contents of the strategic plans are in the internal processes perspective, which is the essence of the strategy. There is clearly room for improvement in the description of the objectives in the customer and financial perspectives.

The experiences of this study testify to the applicability of the Balanced Scorecard approach in the evaluation of strategic plans even though the approach has not been used in the planning or implementation of the strategic plans. The Balanced Scorecard approach can be successfully used to create strategic awareness among the personnel of the libraries and align the defined objectives with the network and the home institution. The perspectives of the Balanced Scorecard can be used to better understand the objectives and their causal relationships.

The main obstacle to making network strategic plans is the difficulty in defining the objectives to which library is able to commit. The additional funding from the Ministry has created incentives for the libraries to define the joint objectives enabling the cooperation and necessary investments. This is a systematic approach to use scarce resources and increase the cost-efficiency of the libraries. The libraries of the universities of applied sciences successfully adapt their strategies to the education policy and changing environment.

References

Adeyoyin, S.O. (2005), "Strategic planning for marketing library services", *Library Management*, Vol. 26 No. 8/9, pp. 494-507.

AMKIT Consortimm (2007), AMKIT Consortium, available at: http://www.amkit.fi/index.php?eng (accessed 8 April 2007).

Bawden, D. (2001), "Information and digital literacies: A review of concepts", *Journal of Documentation*, Vol. 57 No. 2, pp. 218-259.

Breeding, M. (2006), "Reshuffling the Deck", *Library Journal*, available at: http://www.libraryjournal.com/article/CA6319048.html (accessed 9 February 2007)

Bush, T. and Coleman, M. (2000), *Leadership and Strategic Management in Education*, Paul Chapman Publishing, London.

Davies, B. and Ellison, L. (2003), *The New Strategic Direction and Development of the School*, Routledge Falmer, London.

Decker, R. and Höppner, M. (2006), "Strategic planning and customer intelligence in academic libraries", *Library Hi Tech*, Vol. 24 No. 4, pp. 504-514.

Fidler, B. (2002), *Strategic Management for School Development*, Paul Chapman Publishing, London.

Frumkin, J. (2004), "The problem of mainstreaming digital libraries", *OCLC Systems & Services*, Vol. 20 No. 3, pp. 106-109.

Gallimore, A. (1999), "Networked public library", *Library Management*, Vol. 20 No. 7, pp. 384-392.

Guy, F. (2000), "Progress towards the development of digital libraries: The experiences of some national libraries in North America, Australasia and Europe", *Russian Digital Libraries Journal*, Vol. 3 No. 3, available at: http://www.elbib.ru/index.phtml?page=elbib/eng/journal/2000/part3/guy (accessed 9 February 2007).

Huotari, M.-L. and Iivonen, M. (2005), "Knowledge processes: A strategic foundation for the partnership between the university and its library", *Library Management*, Vol. 26 No. 6/7, pp. 324-335.

Jin, Y. (2004), "The development of the China networked digital library of theses and dissertations", *Online Information Review*, Vol. 28 No. 5, pp. 367-370.

Johnson, G. and Scholes, K. (2002), *Exploring Corporate Strategy: Text and Cases*, Prentice Hall, Cambridge.

Kaplan, R.S. and Norton, D.P. (1996), *The Balanced Scorecard*, Harvard Business School Press, Boston, MA.

Kaplan, R.S. and Norton, D.P. (2001), *The Strategy-Focused Organization*, Harvard Business School Press, Boston, MA.

Kaplan, R.S. and Norton, D.P. (2004), *Strategy Maps*, Harvard Business School Press, Boston, MA.

Kettunen, J. (2003), "Strategic evaluation by students in higher education", *Perspectives: Policy and Practice in Higher Education*, Vol. 7 No. 1, pp. 14-18.

Kettunen, J. (2004a), "The strategic evaluation of regional development in higher education", *Assessment & Evaluation in Higher Education*, Vol. 29 No. 3, pp. 357-368.

Kettunen, J. (2004b), "Bridge building for the future of Finnish polytechnics", *Journal of Higher Education Outreach and Engagement*, Vol. 9 No. 2, pp. 43-57.

Kettunen, J. (2005), "Implementation of strategies in continuing education", *The International Journal of Educational Management*, Vol. 19, No. 3, pp. 207-217.

Liu, Y.Q. (2004), "Is the education on digital libraries adequate?", *New Library World*, Vol. 105 No. 1/2, pp. 60-68.

Lloyd, A. (2003), "Information literacy: The meta-competency of the knowledge economy? An exploratory paper", *Journal of Librarianship and Information Science*, Vol. 35 No. 2, pp. 87-92.

Nagata, H., Satoh, Y., Gerrard, S. and Kytömäki, P. (2004), "The dimensions that construct the evaluation of service quality in academic libraries", *Performance Measurement and Metrics*, Vol. 5 No. 2, pp. 53-65.

O'Neil, H.F.Jr., Besimon, E.M., Diamond, M.A. and Moore, M.R. (1999), "Designing and implementing an academic scorecard", *Change*, Vol. 31 No. 6, pp. 32-40.

Owusu-Ansah, E.K. (2003), "Information literacy and academic library: A critical look at a concept and the controversies surrounding it", *The Journal of Academic Librarianship*, Vol. 29 No. 4, pp. 219-230.

Pace, A.K. (2004), "Dismantling integrated library systems", *Library Journal*, available at: http://libraryjournal.com/article/CA374953.html (accessed 9 February 2007).

Poll, R. (2001), "Performance measures for library networked services and resources", *The Electronic Library*, Vol. 19 No. 5, pp. 307-315.

Porter, M. (1996), "What is strategy?" *Harvard Business Review*, November-December, pp. 61-78.

Rowley, J. (2005), "Making sense of the quality maze: perspectives for public and academic libraries", *Library Management*, Vol. 26 No. 8/9, pp. 508-518.

Sharma, R.K. and Vishwanathan, K.R. (2001), "Digital libraries: development and challenges", *Library Review*, Vol. 50 No. 1, pp. 10-16.

Tam, L.W.H. (2000), "Quality management theory and practice: some observations of practices in Australian academic libraries", *Library Management*, Vol. 21 No. 7, pp. 349-356.

V. Strategic Planning of Regional Development in Higher Education

1. Introduction

The Finnish Ministry of Education in June 2004 asked all the higher education institutions (HEIs) in Finland to plan joint regional strategies to increase their external impact on their respective regions. In Finland there where then 20 traditional universities and 29 polytechnics. The strategies have been planned mainly for the regions, but the HEIs in the sparsely populated parts of the country, East and North Finland, planned the strategies for larger geographical areas. The plans were made by the end of September 2005 in cooperation with the authorities responsible for regional development.

The HEIs try to adapt their resources, activities and knowledge to the changing environment. The changes in the environment include globalization, ageing of the population, increasing information technology, internationalisation of education and research, changing interdependence in the regions, and regional networks and cooperation. The regional strategic plans of the institutions also take into account the increasing cooperation of municipalities in the regions and the differentiation of the regions.

The strategy can be seen as the direction and scope of an organisation in the future (Johnson and Scholes, 2002). The strategic plan is a holistic and shared understanding of how the organisation achieves the desired future position. The educational institutions need to adapt their activities to education policy and a changing environment. The strategy can also be planned for a network of cooperative and otherwise independent organisations. The network strategies gather and align resources of various organisations to achieve the shared strategic objective.

The regions typically emphasise the strategy of focusing their resources and attention on their strengths and the most promising fields to create economic growth and welfare for their residents and companies. Another typical strategy of regions features the operations excellence in many different ways. They try to increase their production and improve quality. The third strategy is the differentiation of the regions based on their competitive advantage. These general strategies presented by Porter (1990, 1996) can be applied in various ways in regional development.

This purpose of this chapter is to present the regional network strategies and show that the Balanced Scorecard approach can be successfully used in the description and communication of network strategies. The Balanced Scorecard was developed by Kaplan and Norton (1992, 1993) and has been applied worldwide in companies and public organisations. The study presents the case of seven HEIs in Turku, which is located in the middle of the Baltic Sea Region. The institutions planned a joint regional strategy for the region of Southwest Finland (Higher Education Institutions in Turku, 2005).

The HEIs decided on their joint strategic plan to develop their strengths and avoid overlapping support services, education and research and development (R&D). This enables them to allocate resources and activities to regional development. The engagement and outreach of institutions aims to improve the competitive advantage, economic growth, employment and welfare of the region. Internationalisation and increased entrepreneurship have also been selected as specific themes in the regional strategy.

This chapter is organised as follows: Section 2 presents the characteristics of the strategic planning of HEIs. Section 3 describes how the Balanced Scorecard approach can be used in the description of the strategy. Section 4 describes the strategic initiatives to implement the regional strategy. Finally, the results of the study are summarised and discussed in the concluding section.

2. Strategic planning

Mission and vision

The strategic plan describes the route from the present position described by the mission to the desirable future position described by the vision (Wheale, 1991; West-Burnham, 1994). For an educational institution it is a holistic and shared understanding of how it adapts to education policy, environment and develops its activities for a better future (Middlewood and Lumby, 1998, Bush and Coleman, 2000).

A challenge of network strategies is to involve a sufficient number of managers and individuals, at least in part, in the strategy process. The commitment is especially important in knowledge and service work, where individuals have great power to subvert, constrain or ignore changes that they do not accept (Drucker, 1994). All the participants of the network must involve a sufficient number of people and communicate the joint strategic plans efficiently to ensure their implementation.

The regional strategy was planned by a working group with representatives from all the HEIs in the region, the City of Turku, the Turku Chamber of Commerce, the State Provincial Office of Western Finland, the Employment and Economic Development Centre for Southwest Finland and the Regional Council of Southwest Finland. The working group also took into account the opinions of a larger group of experts. The group met 12 times to complete the strategic plan. The plan was discussed in the various management groups of the institutions and detailed action plans were made. Finally the plans were approved at the respective boards of the institutions by the end of September 2005.

The mission statement of an organisation defines its primary purpose or the reason why it has been established. The mission is regarded as a specific expression for the organisation's present activities (Kettunen, 2003). The mission statement is a relatively stable concept, which motivates the employees to work on behalf of the main purpose of the organisation. The mission can also articulate the main responsibilities of an organisation to its customers and society.

The mission statement of the HEIs in the regional strategic plan is written as follows:

The HEIs in Turku participate in regional development of Southwest Finland as the producer of research knowledge and skilled labour and the mediator of knowledge, creativeness and know-how. The HEIs cooperate according to their own tasks and profiles in close cooperation with each other and other main actors of regional development.

The mission is consistent with the laws of traditional universities and the polytechnics, which stipulate the tasks of institutions in a more specific way. The Universities Act stipulates that the societal impact is the "third task" of the universities and complements education and research. The Polytechnics Act stipulates that applied R&D supports regional development. Both of these laws emphasise the outreach and engagement of the HEIs in their environments.

The vision statement is an expression about the desired future state of an organisation. The strategic plan requires an explicit description of the intended direction and state in which an organisation is moving from its present situation (Fidler, 2002; Davies and Ellison, 2003). A well-expressed vision should be inspirational, clear and challenging (Peters, 1988). The vision should motivate the members of the organisation to work in the desired direction with pride and enthusiasm.

The vision statement of the regional strategic plan of the HEIs in Turku is written as follows:

The HEIs in Turku form a high-quality and internationally known centre of higher education and R&D, which is based on multidisciplinary knowledge, close cooperation and profile-based work sharing. It supports and promotes the welfare of the region, economic growth and diverse cultural life.

The vision emphasises the external effects of the HEIs on regional development based on the outlines of the Ministry of Education. The HEIs will focus on the development of their strengths, which is the basis for the work-sharing and close cooperation with each other. The institutions also aim to increase their external influence on their environment.

Strategic themes

Strategic themes describe the strategy of an organisation in a concise way. They express what the decision makers believe must be done to succeed and achieve the desired objectives (Kaplan and Norton, 2001). An organisation's objectives tend to emerge as the wishes of the most dominant coalition (Cyert and March, 1963). The strategic themes and objectives form a coherent and consistent plan of how to develop the organisation towards the vision. Strategic themes are unique to the organisations' environment and situation in which the strategy was planned.

The Ministry of Education in June 2004 imposed a requirement that Finnish HEIs plan regional strategies. The strengths of each institution were defined to facilitate work-sharing and cooperation between institutions in order to increase the external regional impact of the institutions. The regional strategies were planned by the end of September 2005. According to the plan, the Ministry will fund the strategic initiatives and award prizes for the best plans.

The guidelines of the Ministry of Education follow the cost-efficiency and focus strategies. The HEIs should cooperate with each other, reduce their overlapping activities and unnecessary costs. The HEIs should also allocate their resources to research, development and other activities to increase the external impact. They should focus their activities to create competitiveness for economic growth and increase residents' well-being. These are actually competitive strategies presented by Porter (1990, 1996) and they can also be used in educational institutions and non-profit organisations (Treacy and Wiersema, 1995; Kettunen, 2002, 2005).

The strategic themes were planned in line with the guidelines of the Ministry of Education. The strategic themes are written as follows:

• *Societal responsibility. The institutions will cooperatively develop the welfare, social and cultural capital and sustainable development of the region.*
• *Internationalisation. The institutions will promote the internationalisation of the region and develop the international cooperation.*
• *Entrepreneurship. The institutions will cooperatively develop entrepreneurship, entrepreneurship education and the operational preconditions of companies in the region.*

• *Cooperation of HEIs. The institutions will strengthen their mutual cooperation for the benefit of the region.*

The first strategic theme emphasises the outreach and engagement of the institutions in their region. The purpose of this theme is that the institutions define their focal areas where they aim to increase their external impact on their environments. The external impact is a result of intensified cooperation between the institutions, which is described in the last strategic theme. The strategic plan clearly aims to put an end to the era of ivory towers.

The second strategic theme aims to strengthen the international activities of the institutions and to internationalise the region. Internationalisation is important, because Finland is a small open economy, in which the foreign trade has an important role. The theme of internationalisation also aims to develop the Baltic Sea Region and increase cooperation between Nordic Countries.

The third strategic theme aims to increase entrepreneurship in the region. The institutions are committed to increasing entrepreneurship education, research and other activities. Entrepreneurship can be seen as a driving force to generate economic activity and welfare in the region. On the other hand, it supports the theme of internationalisation, because entrepreneurship is for immigrants often the only way to obtain employment.

The last strategic theme emphasises the cooperation of educational institutions. The strengthening of the focal areas of educational institutions and removing of the overlapping activities will enable them to allocate increased resources to R&D and other activities that support regional development. The strengthening of strengths is the basis for the natural cooperation between the institutions.

3. The Balanced Scorecard describes the strategy

The perspectives of the Balanced Scorecard

The Balanced Scorecard approach translates the strategic plan into tangible objectives and locates them into different perspectives to describe the functioning of an organisation (Kaplan and Norton, 1996). Typically management balances the objectives of the strategy in four perspectives including customer, finance, internal processes and learning. The approach helps management to communicate the strategy to the employees and other stakeholders. The balancing of objectives helps management to communicate how the organisation operates, how it can achieve the objectives and who is responsible for the achievement of the targets in the planning period.

Organisations that are managed using measurement systems tend to have better teamwork at the top level, better communication at all levels and better self-management at the lowest level (Lingle and Shieman, 1996). Frigo and Krumwiede (1999) have also found evidence that performance management systems based on the Balanced Scorecard are significantly more effective compared to other systems.

The perspectives of the Balanced Scorecard can be defined in the regional strategy of HEIs in Turku as follows:

1. Regional development. The regional development perspective includes the objectives which describe the institutions' outreach and engagement in regional development. The achievement of these objectives is the result of processes and structures.

2. Customer. The customer perspective includes the objectives related to residents or customer organisations. These outcomes can also be achieved as the results of processes and structures.

3. Finance. The financial perspective describes the joint financial objectives of the HEIs. Finance should always be aligned with the processes and structures.

4. Processes and structures. This perspective describes the sequential processes including the processes of support service and the block of processes including education and R&D. Education and R&D cannot be separated from each other in the strategic plan.

5. Learning. The learning perspective includes the drivers for the future performance described in the processes and structures perspective.

In this case the perspective describing the desired objectives was divided into regional development and customer services to address the institutions' relationship with their environment. It is reasonable to place the regional development and customer perspectives at the top of the hierarchy, because the financial result is not the primary purpose of institutions as in business companies. The regional development and customer perspectives are similar, because they are results of the processes and structures. In many other cases they have been combined in a customer perspective.

Strategy maps

The strategy map is a graphical representation of the strategy, which includes the objectives of the perspectives and their causal relationships (Kaplan and Norton, 2001, 2004). It helps the management of the organisation to communicate the strategy to the employees and stakeholders and to articulate why the objectives have been set and how they can be achieved. The strategy maps, like a road map, illustrate the main characteristics of the strategy on the way to the better future described by the vision.

Figure 1 presents the strategy map of the HEIs in Turku. It is a general representation of the relationships between the objectives in the perspectives. The learning perspective includes the performance drivers. The regional development and customer perspectives include the desired objectives. These are results of the activities in the processes and structures perspective. The financial objectives must be aligned with the objectives of the processes and structures in the budgeting process.

The regional development perspective includes five objectives regarding the HEIs' outreach and engagement in their environment. The institutions aim to strengthen their cooperation in the Nordic Countries and participate to establish a Centre of the Baltic Sea together with the City of Turku and the Regional Council of Southwest Finland. It is supported by the internationalisation of the region. The HEIs will also continue their cooperation in Southwest Finland. They aim to provide higher education and other activities in different parts of the region. They also aim to develop the innovation environment and technology transfer, especially in the Turku Science Park. The promotion of cultural activities is also a regional objective, because it strengthens the identity of the region, promotes the well-being of residents and helps the companies to relocate to the region.

The customer perspective includes three objectives, which are related to creating value and achieving customer satisfaction. The HEIs aim to promote societal responsibility and sustainable development for which there are special units at the Turku School of Economics and Business Administration and specific activities at Turku Polytechnic. The HEIs aim to improve the health care, social services and social capital of residents. They also aim to develop small and medium-sized companies and to support the change of enterprises to the next generation.

The financial perspective includes two objectives to be achieved to fund the internal processes and structures. The HEIs will take advantage of the national, Nordic and European funding sources in R&D with joint efforts. The centres of continuing education plan regionally efficient joint projects financed through various funding programmes and aim especially at international cooperation. Many of the activities of the strategy are financed by reallocating the basic funding from central government in the budgets of the institutions.

The processes and structures perspective includes the blocks "support services" and "education and R&D" in the strategy map. The support services describe the joint structures which have been planned to support education and R&D. The joint support services are planned to reduce overlapping costs and produce more efficient services enabling the allocation of resources to increase the external impact of the institutions. The block education and R&D includes the main activities of the institutions, which should have an external impact on regional development.

Figure 1. Strategy map of the HEIs in Turku

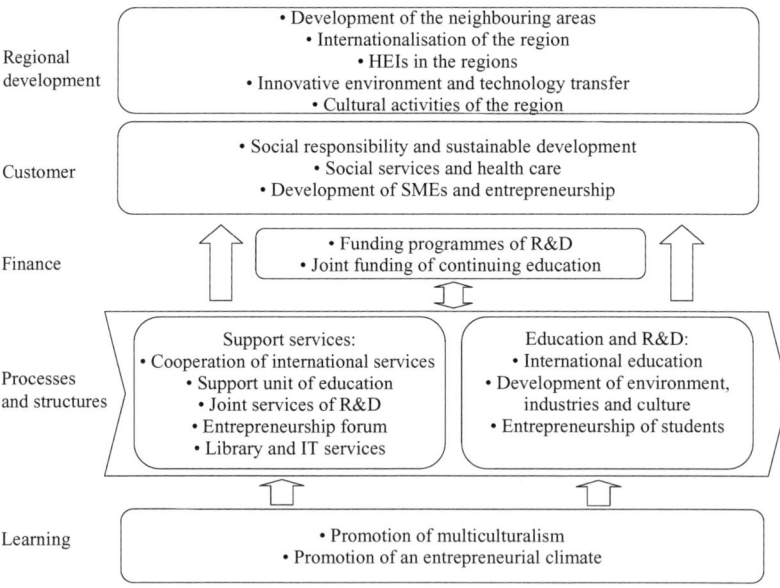

The block "support services" in the strategy map includes five objectives. The institutions will establish a working group to develop the international cooperation of the institutions and work in close cooperation with other regional units responsible for international affairs. The institutions will establish a permanent cooperation group to support the coordination of education. The institutions will strengthen cooperation in research and technology transfer. They will also establish an entrepreneurship forum to develop their cooperation with local companies. They will also strengthen their cooperation with libraries, information technology services and other facilities.

The block "education and R&D" includes three objectives including joint activities supporting regional development. The institutions aim to increase international education and student exchange in fields that support the internationalisation of the region. The institutions will increase their cooperation in environmental issues, industrial development and cultural life. The institutions will also promote entrepreneurship among students and the new business in the region.

The learning perspective includes two objectives supporting internationalisation and entrepreneurship. The objective of multiculturalism aims to achieve a positive attitude to immigrants and help them relocate in Finnish society so that they can become employed and establish new companies. The institutions also aim to promote the culture and climate of entrepreneurship in cooperation with the public sector and other organisations. Positive attitudes to internationalisation and entrepreneurship are the drivers of future performance in these activities.

4. Strategic initiatives to implement the strategy

The purpose of the strategic initiatives is to achieve a substantial cost reduction or quality improvement in order to satisfy regional or customer needs. According to the guidelines by the Ministry of Education the strategic plan of the HEIs should include three strategic initiatives with financial plans. In 2006 the HEIs jointly planned three initiatives and applied the Ministry of Education for funding.

HEIs in the regions

This is a cooperative project of the University of Turku, Turku Polytechnic, the Turku School of Economics and Business Administration, Åbo Akademi University, the Diaconia Polytechnic, the Humanities Polytechnic and the Sydväst Polytechnic in the regions of Loimaa, Salo, Turunmaa and Vakka-Suomi. The project is a response to the development needs of the regions. The project supports the strategic objective of the "regional HEI", which is included in the strategic theme emphasising the cooperation of institutions.

The purpose of the project is to provide the regions with know-how, education and R&D services so as to meet the needs of the companies, municipalities and residents in a flexible and customer-oriented manner. The purpose is also to improve the competitiveness of the organisations and activate the regional operators to create joint development networks. One possibility is to take advantage of the digital learning environments in the distance education of the Open University and continuing education.

The Centre for Child and Youth Research

Turku Polytechnic, the Turku School of Economics and Business Administration, the University of Turku, the Sydväst Polytechnic, Åbo Akademi University, the Diaconia Polytechnic and the Humanities Polytechnic are participating in the project. The project responds to the diversified development needs of the care of children and young people. The project supports the strategic objective of "social services and health care" in the strategic theme of societal responsibility.

The purpose is to establish the Centre for Child and Youth Research. The centre will promote the R&D of the institutions so that it has a decisive effect on the region and society. The project will create models for cooperation with the municipalities and other stakeholders to ensure the transfer of know-how. This is a multi-disciplinary project, which includes specialists in health care, social welfare, education and culture.

Treatment chains in health care

The University of Turku, Turku Polytechnic, the Sydväst Polytechnic and the Hospital District of Southwest Finland and health centres in the region participate in this project. It responds to the increasing demand for health services in Southwest Finland due to the ageing of its population. This project also supports the strategic objective of "social services and health care" in the strategic theme of societal responsibility.

The purpose of the project is to achieve the objective of health promotion. It will provide opportunities for the professionals in health care to upgrade their know-how. The project includes multi-professional cooperation in education between the institutions. It also supports the interaction of educational institutions and working life and promotes the matching of the users of health services and professionals. The project will also develop a digital learning environment for use in the various regions.

The strategic initiatives have been planned to implement the network strategy of regional development. When the network strategy has been planned jointly between the HEIs it is advisable to implement the strategy in cooperation between the selected institutions using the strategic initiatives. The knowledge and know-how of the participating institutions complement each other in these projects. The participation of the institutions is based on their strengths thereby facilitating their cooperation.

The strategic initiatives are not the only means to implement the network strategy. Each institution has its own overall strategies defining general outlines for regional development. Some institutions may also have their own regional strategies, which are specific to their activities in regional development. Turku Polytechnic has defined its own regional strategic plan, which aims to meet the development of regions in Southwest Finland.

5. Conclusions

Some decades ago the traditional universities in Finland emphasised their autonomy and avoided direct contacts with companies and other organisations. However, the education policy has changed in the 21st century. In June 2004 The Ministry of Education imposed a requirement that the HEIs in each region should increase their cooperation and plan their regional strategies by the end of September 2005. This is a systematic attempt to utilise meagre resources more efficiently. The purpose is to avoid overlapping operations, improve the strengths of institutions and allocate resources to regional development.

All the traditional universities and the polytechnics planned their regional strategies. Most of the strategies were planned for the regions in which the institutions are located. There are also strategic plans for the larger areas in sparsely populated East and North Finland. The quality and contents of the strategic plans are different in the various regions of the country. The Balanced Scorecard approach can also be used as a tool to plan and communicate network strategies for other regions in the Baltic countries.

There has been an obvious need to upgrade the knowledge of strategic management in HEIs and to provide tools to describe and communicate the strategic plans. The Balanced Scorecard approach helps the managers and employees of the HEIs to better understand the strategic plan. It is a useful tool to describe the network strategy of regional development. The network is able to define joint strategic themes that can be taken into account in the strategic themes of the cooperating organisations. The Balanced Scorecard also helps to define joint objectives, which can be allocated to the participating organisations for implementation.

The Balanced Scorecard approach provides managers and employees in each educational institution with a clear understanding of how their work contributes to the network strategy. The ownership of the objectives and measures delegates the responsibility to different institutions. Different administrative units can define their own themes and objectives. The units and individuals can be entrusted with achieving the objectives. This enables the evaluation and adjudication of the implementation of the strategy and the results achieved.

The regional strategy of Southwest Finland has four strategic themes describing societal responsibility, internationalisation, entrepreneurship and cooperation between HEIs. These themes include 21 objectives. Most of the objectives have on-going projects, but also new initiatives were also expected from the different institutions. The strategic plan specified three new joint projects including the project "HEIs in the regions", "the Centre of Child and Youth Research" and "treatment chains in health care". These development projects are to be funded by the Ministry of Education.

References

Bush, T. and Coleman, M. (2000). Leadership and Strategic Management in Education. London: Paul Chapman Publishing.

Cyert, R.M. and March, J.G. (1963). Behavioral Theory of the Firm. Englewood Cliffs, NJ: Prentice-Hall.

Davies, B. and Ellison, L. (2003). The New Strategic Direction and Development of the School. London: Routledge Falmer.

Drucker, P. (1994). The Theory of Business, Harvard Business Review, September-October, 95-104.

Fidler, B. (2002). Strategic Management for School Development. London: Paul Chapman Publishing.

Frigo, M.L. and Krumwiede, K.R. (1999). Balanced Scorecard: A Rising Trend in Strategic Performance Measurement, Journal of Strategic Performance Measurement, February-March, 42-48.

Higher Education Institutions in Turku (2005). Turkulaisten korkeakoulujen alueellisen kehittämisen strategia 2006-2012, Turku.

Johnson, G. and Scholes, K. (2002). Exploring Corporate Strategy: Text and Cases, 6th edition, Cambridge: Prentice Hall.

Kaplan, R. and Norton, D. (1992). The Balanced Scorecard: Measures that Drive Performance, Harvard Business Review, January-February, 71-79.

Kaplan, R. and Norton, D. (1993). Putting the Balanced Scorecard to Work, Harvard Business Review, September-October, 134-147.

Kaplan, R.S. and Norton, D.P. (1996). Translating Strategy into Action, The Balanced Scorecard. Boston, Massachusetts: Harvard Business School Press.

Kaplan, R.S. and Norton, D.P. (2001). The Strategy-Focused Organization, How Balanced Scorecard Companies Thrive in the New Business Environment. Boston, Massachusetts: Harvard Business School Press.

Kaplan, R.S. & Norton, D.P. (2004). Strategy Maps, Converting the Intangible Assets into Tangible Outcomes. Boston, Massachusetts: Harvard Business School Press

Kettunen, J. (2002). Competitive Strategies in Higher Education, Journal of Institutional Research 11, 38-47.

Kettunen, J. (2003). Strategic Evaluation of Institutions by Students in Higher Education, Perspectives: Policy and Practice in Higher Education 7, 14-18.

Kettunen, J. (2005). Implementation of Strategies in Continuing Education, The International Journal of Educational Management 19 (3), 207-217.

Lingle, J.H. and Shieman, W.A. (1996). From Balanced Scorecards to Strategic Gauges: Is Measurement Worth It? Management Review, March, 56-62.

Middlewood, D. and Lumby, J. (1998). Strategic Management in Schools and Colleges. London: Paul Chapman Publishing Ltd.

Peters, T. (1988). Thriving on Chaos. New York: Alfred A. Knopf.

Porter, M. (1990). The Competitive Advantage of Nations. London: Macmillan.

Porter, M. (1996). What is Strategy? Harvard Business Review, November-December, 61-78.

Treacy M. and Wiersema, F. (1995). The Discipline of Market Leaders: Choose Your Customers, Narrow Your Focus, Dominate Your Market. Reading, MA: Addison-Wesley.

West-Burnham, J. (1994). Strategy, policy and planning, in Bush, T. and West-Burnham, J. (Eds.), The Principles of Educational Management, Longman: Harlow, 77-99.

Wheale, J. (1991). Generating Income for Educational Institutions: A Business Planning Approach. London: Kogan Page.

VI. The Collective Process and Memory of Strategic Management

1. Introduction

Cities, like many other public sector organizations typically emphasise the strategy of focusing attention and resources on the most promising fields to create economic growth and welfare for their residents. Another typical strategy features the operations excellence theme. The public sector organizations take their mission as given and try to reduce their costs, improve quality and do so more efficiently using their fixed annual budgets. The cost-efficiency strategy means that the organization delivers a combination of costs and quality that is recognised by the taxpayers. These strategies have been presented in a generic form by Porter (1990, 1996).

There are numerous variations regarding the focus and cost-efficiency strategies, because they are unique to the organization and its environment. Managing cities in complex and changing environments is a demanding task. The effective implementation of strategies should affect the behaviour of people in the organization. Skilled managers try to process information from a large number of indicators to manage their organization. There is a need for rational measures of accountability and effectiveness in the public sector.

Budgeting is the primary management system in most public organizations. The financial objectives of an organization should be aligned and linked together with the other objectives of strategic planning, because financial objectives are critical in achieving non-financial objectives. If financial resources remain remote from the other objectives, the organization will not function in a consistent and coherent way to achieve the desired outcomes. In most cases the financial objectives can be achieved by allocating the existing funding in a new way.

The Balanced Scorecard approach was developed by Kaplan and Norton (1992, 1993, 1996). It is a representation of the organization's shared vision and strategy. The Balanced Scorecard helps the organization to define its strategic objectives and measures which communicate the direction of the organization to the desired future state and translate the strategy into action. The strategy must be communicated and understood before it can be implemented.

A city is a complex federation of quasi-independent entities with varying levels of discretion right down to the "street-level bureaucrat" endowing individuals with considerable amount of power. The Balanced Scorecard enables the cities to bridge a major gap between the strategy and its implementation. It enables the management of the cities to establish and communicate the direction to the future both at the citywide and lower organizational levels. The decision-makers should achieve a consensus among themselves about what their vision and strategy mean. An important barrier to the implementation of the strategy is that the organization cannot translate the strategy into action if it cannot be understood by those persons who are going to implement it.

The purpose of this chapter is to show how strategic management can be integrated with the traditional budgeting in the cities at the various organizational levels. The study presents the case of the City of Turku, which is located in Southwest Finland in the middle of the Baltic Sea Region. The City Council has decided in its strategy to improve its competitive advantage and the sustainable development of the region. It also emphasises the welfare and quality of life. In addition it wants to emphasise the role of education, knowledge creation and entrepreneurship as driving forces for a better future.

The study presents more detailed the case of the Turku University of Applied Sciences, which has planned and implemented a management information system tailored to utilise its various information systems and meet the requirements of the management process. The data warehouse transforms various source data and provides reliable information to users of the portal. This system supports managers in their programme monitoring and planning tasks. However, the system is more than a traditional management scorecard. It is an electronic platform which effectively supports the integration of strategic planning, continuous improvement and the building of organizational memory (Takeuchi and Nonaka, 1995, 2004). The management portal includes strategic plans, which are then translated into more concrete budgets and annual action and human resource plans.

This chapter is organized as follows: The next section presents the strategic approach to the management of public sector organizations. Then the chapter describes an application of how the Balanced Scorecard can be developed for large city organizations to promote economic growth and welfare in a region. Then the chapter presents a general framework of how the Balanced Scorecard can be integrated into budgeting to implement the strategy and create the common organizational memory. Finally, the results of the study are summarized and discussed in the concluding section.

2. Strategic planning

Mission, vision and values

Strategy is the direction and scope of an organization over the long term. It matches the resources to the changing environment, markets and customers to meet the expectations of stakeholders (Johnson and Scholes, 2002; Steiss, 2003). Public sector organizations are moving from the traditional public orientation to the market orientation, which emphasises the role of strategic management (Joldersma and Winter, 2002). The management of cities has also moved in an entrepreneurial direction (Jessop and Sum, 2000).

A great challenge for large cities is to involve a sufficient number of managers and personnel, at least in part, in the strategy process. The participation of elected officials and civil servants in a well-planned strategy process can be seen as more important than the final strategic plan. This is especially true in knowledge and service work, where individuals have great power to subvert, constrain or ignore changes that they do not accept (Drucker, 1994). Typically the planning period of cities is the term for which officials are elected to serve, which is four years in Finland. The strategy process should produce the mission, vision, values and strategic themes for the planning period.

The City Council of Turku introduced the Balanced Scorecard approach first time 2002 to communicate and implement the strategic plan of the election period 2001-2004. The next strategy process lead by the City Council started just after the municipal elections in October 2004. The elected officials and civil servants conducted a thorough process at many levels of the city organization. The process also took into account the opinions and advice of external stakeholders such as universities, companies and the Association of Local and Regional Authorities. The strategy process produced the strategic plan for the period 2005 - 2008. The plan was approved by the City Council in May 2005 and during the autumn it was integrated with the budget in the period 2006 – 2008.

The mission of an organization defines the primary purpose or the reason why the organization has been established. The mission is a relatively stable concept, which is regarded as a specific expression for the organization's present activities. It should motivate the employees to work and promote the main purpose of an organization. The mission also articulates the responsibilities of an organization to its customers and stakeholders (Kettunen, 2003). The mission statement of the City of Turku is written as follows:

Turku is a bilingual growth centre in the Baltic Sea are and the leading city in the economic region, focusing on regional co-operation. The city's assets are its history, its multicultural, international background, its logistic position and its dedication to innovative work and sustainable development.

Turku provides a safe environment to live in, competitive high-quality services for both inhabitants and businesses, and conditions tailored to meet the requirements of trade and industry.

The city bases its activities on municipal democracy, resident and customer orientation, a committed personnel and a high-level competence.

The core of the mission is that the City of Turku serves its residents with high quality and improves the conditions for business life. It can be seen that the mission is rather long and may need shortening in the future.

The desired future state of an organization is expressed by the vision. Strategic planning requires an explicit description how an organization is moving from the present day described by the mission in the intended direction and state (Fidler, 2002; Davies and Ellison, 2003). A well-expressed vision should be simple, short and understandable and it should motivate the members of the organization to work towards it with pride and enthusiasm. The vision statement of the City of Turku for 2015 is written as follows:

Finland's oldest city, Turku, is a nationally and internationally attractive city of culture and a competence centre providing an excellent quality of life and an innovative environment for work.

The implication of the vision is that the cultural activities and education should be developed in the future to profile the city in this direction. The vision statement is clearly shorter and more concise than the mission statement. Therefore it is easier to remember in everyday work.

Every organization has its own characteristic spirit. The culture of an organization is the collection of beliefs, expectations and values shared by the organization's members and transmitted from one generation of employees to another (Wheelen and Hunger, 1995). The values may be implicit patterns of thought, which underpin the behaviour and attitudes of individuals within organizations and they should be in line with the mission of an organization (Schein, 1985). The explicit values can be used for the guiding the workers and decision-makers in an organization's strategy to achieve the vision.

The values of the City of Turku have been unchanged for a decade. The values are written as follows:
- *resident and customer orientation*
- *competence and creativity*
- *sustainable development*
- *justice*
- *co-operation.*

The values are used in decision-making and when the outlines for the operation are sought. It is, however, a challenge in a large and diverse organization of 13 000 workers to make these values better known.

Strategic themes

The cities and other municipalities typically emphasise strategic themes of focus and cost-efficiency. The municipalities focus their political attention and resources on specific operations which are the most promising fields to create competitiveness for economic growth to improve residents' well-being. The focus strategy enables the cities to make strategic choices and enhance their knowledge and improve quality in the selected segments.

The municipalities also try to reduce their costs and improve efficiency on shoestring budgets. Cost efficiency is a natural choice, because the municipalities typically have relatively fixed amount of tax-income. Cost-efficient municipalities deliver an efficient combination of costs and quality. The municipalities try to eliminate overlapping activities so as to avoid unnecessary costs. The cost-efficiency strategy makes it possible to focus on specific activities, which means that cost-efficiency and focus strategies complement each other. These generic competitive strategies have been presented by Porter (1990, 1996) for business companies but they can also be used in non-profit organizations (Treacy and Wiersema, 1995; Kettunen, 2002, 2005).

The strategy of an organization can be described using strategic themes in a concise way. The strategic themes of a municipality describe what the decision-makers and administrators believe must be done to succeed and achieve the desired outcomes. The strategic themes are linked to the organization's internal processes and the opportunities to create value for customers in a changing environment. Each organization has a unique set of strategic themes planned for its situation.

The elected officials and leading administrators prepared the strategic themes thoroughly and eventually selected the following three specific themes:
• *Competitiveness and sustainable development*
• *Well-being and quality of life*
• *Vitality through education, competence and entrepreneurship*

The first strategic theme aims to increase the competitive advantage of the region and achieve the desired results for its environment. The second theme emphasises the value for residents which is a result of the efficient service processes. The third theme aims to increase the economic growth which is based on the knowledge and skills provided by educational institutions.

The theme of competitiveness and sustainable development includes seven objectives. The City Council commits to city structure that supports sustainable development and well-being. The Council also aims at cost-efficient and resident-oriented activities and balanced economy. The city will be the leader of regional co-operation and an active guardian of interests. It will be a notable international actor and a powerful force in the development of the Baltic Sea Region. The City Council also aims at a responsible climate and environment policy.

The theme of well-being and quality of life has four objectives. The City Council aims to develop the conditions of children, young people and families with children. The Council will promote health and freedom from obstacles and support for life control and individual activity. Turku will be a lively and creative city of culture. It also will have a resident-oriented service production and developing partnership.

The theme of vitality through education, competence and entrepreneurship has three objectives. The City of Turku will have creative and high-level education. The City Council will develop the co-operation between higher education institutions and companies to support innovativeness. It also will support the diversification of the economic structure and the growth industries.

3. The Balanced Scorecard communicates and implements the strategy

The perspectives of the Balanced Scorecard

Organizations that are managed using measurement systems tend to have better teamwork at the top, better communication throughout the organization and better self-management at the lowest level (Lingle and Shieman, 1996). There is also evidence that performance management systems based on the Balanced Scorecard are significantly more effective compared to other systems (Frigo and Krumwiede, 1999).

The Balanced Scorecard approach translates the strategy into tangible objectives located in the different perspectives. The objectives are described using measures and their target values. The approach helps management to communicate the strategy to the employees and other stakeholders. The balancing of objectives needs an "organizational theory" about how the organization can achieve the desired outcomes. Usually the objectives are balanced in four perspectives including customer, finance, internal processes and learning.

The environment and circumstances of an organization may require one or more additional perspectives. The customer perspective especially may need to be rethought for public organizations. The true customers of public organizations are not only the recipients of public services but the public at large, who benefit from output created by the organizations. The senior personnel of the City of Turku discussed whether the four perspectives were adequate and appropriate for the city's scorecard. The customer perspective was divided into the societal impact perspective to address the city's relationship with society and the customer perspective to address customer satisfaction.

The Balanced Scorecard was originally developed for business companies, but with slight modifications it can also be used in the public sector. The approach has been used in many municipalities such as the City of Charlotte (Kaplan and Norton, 1996) and the Larvik Municipality in Norway (Askim, 2004). The financial perspective typically includes the desired outcomes in the private sector, but in the public sector it is reasonable to place the recipient of the services at the top of the perspectives. In municipalities the taxpayer provides the financial resources and the resident receives the service. It is reasonable to place the societal impact and customer perspectives at the top of the hierarchy, because the financial result is not the primary objective.

The perspectives of the Balanced Scorecard are defined by the City Council as follows:

1. Societal impact. The societal impact perspective includes the objectives which describe the city's effects on society and the local community. They are the results of the city's processes.

2. Customer. The customer perspective includes the objectives of customer satisfaction. These outcomes are the results of the processes.

3. Finance. The financial perspective describes the objectives of cost efficiency and balanced economy. In the budget finance is aligned with the processes.

4. Processes and structures. This perspective describes the sequential processes, which include international and regional development, city planning and efficient services.

5. Learning. The learning perspective includes the drivers for efficient processes and future performance.

The societal impact and customer perspectives are similar. They are external effects of the processes. They describe the outreach and engagement of the city in its region. An alternative would be to use only the customer perspective and include regional development in it as an objective.

The introduction of the Balanced Scorecard

The overall strategy of the City of Turku suffered from a lack of integration with the strategies of the operating units during the planning period 2001 - 2004, because strategies had been planned in some isolation from each other. The implementation of the overall strategy was difficult and frustrating, because it was not comprehensive and lacked linkages to the operative units. Attempts to plan the strategies at operative units lost the opportunity of value-creation from the integration and coordination of unit strategies. Operating units tried to justify their strategies and sought far-fetched linkages with the city strategy.

The City Council of Turku took a decision to implement the strategy using the Balanced Scorecard in 2002. The Council had at that time a fully established strategic plan, but the elected officials and administrators felt that the communication and implementation of the strategy needed more powerful tools. The mission and vision statements and strategic choices communicated the City Council's desire to increase economic growth and serve its residents. The City Council allocated additional financial resources to the strategic choices that would have the greatest impact on the economic growth and well-being of its residents. The elected officials, the Mayor, the Deputy Mayors and Directors of the operative units planned the introduction of the Balanced Scorecard at several meetings. They translated the strategic themes of the existing strategy into strategic objectives and measures. The City Board finally approved the first Balanced Scorecard in May 2002.

There must be integration between the different levels of the overall organization to enable the efficient implementation of the higher level strategies. During the development of the city-level scorecard the Mayor asked all the operative and support units to develop their own Balanced Scorecards. The system enables the operating units' strategies and objectives to contribute to the city's strategic objectives. The directors of operating units were provided guidance, but each operating unit had the responsibility of selecting the measures most appropriate for its particular circumstances.

Some operating units and departments expressed disappointment that their activities did not appear on the scorecard at the overall level. The city-level scorecard cannot represent all the activities and services delivered to its residents. In most cases the operating units also planned the Balanced Scorecards for their departments. The performance of the operating units and their departments is measured against their own objectives. In addition, each of these administrative units plans how its operations contribute to the city-level objectives.

An example of the operating units of the City of Turku is the Turku University of Applied Sciences, where the Balanced Scorecard was built upon the existing performance indicators. The introduction of the Balanced Scorecard was not considered a remarkable change, because the institution already had target values for some indicators. The main contribution of the new system was that it compelled the management to clearly define the objectives and measures, locate them in the perspectives and describe the linkages between the objectives. The other contribution was that the measurement system was enlarged to the department level. The new balanced system was widely accepted, because the employees were better able to see the big picture and the relationships of their jobs to the strategy and objectives of the institutions. The employees' understanding of the organization's objectives is important, because it probably leads to better outcomes, as argued by Rucci, Kirn and Quinn (1998).

Strategy maps

The strategy map is a graphical representation of the strategy developed by Kaplan and Norton (2001, 2004). Like a road map, it illustrates the essential characteristics of the strategy on the way to the better future described by the vision. Strategy maps help the management of the organization to define the objectives and place them in the different perspectives. They also help the employees and stakeholders to understand why the objectives have been set and how they can be achieved.

Figure 1 presents the strategy map of the City of Turku. It describes the perspectives and causal relationships between the perspectives and objectives. The linkages of the strategy map describe the relationships between the performance drivers and the desired outcomes. The achievement of the objectives in the societal impact and customer perspectives is the result of activities in the processes, which require funding and capabilities to implement the necessary processes.

The societal impact perspective includes two objectives namely the "diversified structure of economy and economic growth" of the "clean climate and environment". The customer perspective includes three objectives namely "healthy and active residents", "children, young people and families with children" and "lively and creative cultural life". The societal impact perspective emphasises the city's outreach and engagement in its environment, but the customer perspective is related to the customer satisfaction that virtually all organizations pursue. These objectives are a result of the activities of processes.

The financial perspective includes the objective of the "cost efficiency and balanced economy". The funding from taxpayers, central government and the income from commercial activities are prerequisites to achieve the objectives of the processes. The economic growth of the region must be promoted, because that swells the tax base. The processes must be cost-efficient to ensure sufficient funding. In public sector organizations it is important to achieve a high quality of service with effective activities using minor expenses.

The processes and structures perspective describes the value chain starting from large international and regional objectives and ending with resident-oriented services. The international co-operation is focused on the Baltic Sea Region. Co-operation with other municipalities in Turku Region is important, because more local co-operation helps the municipalities to achieve cost-efficient services. The city planning provides the framework for the infrastructure that supports sustainable growth and welfare. The core of the processes, however, is in resident-oriented service production, which takes advantage of the developing public and private partnership and the regional co-operation to achieve the satisfaction of customers.

The learning perspective includes objectives which are the drivers of future performance. The objectives "co-operation of higher education institutions and companies that support innovativeness" and "creative and high quality education" are prerequisites for efficient processes and structures. The growing and lively cities must have opportunities to improve their capabilities for innovative processes. There are seven higher education institutions in Turku. The City Council strongly emphasises the co-operation of higher education institutions and companies that support the economic growth of the region.

Figure 1. Strategy map of the City of Turku

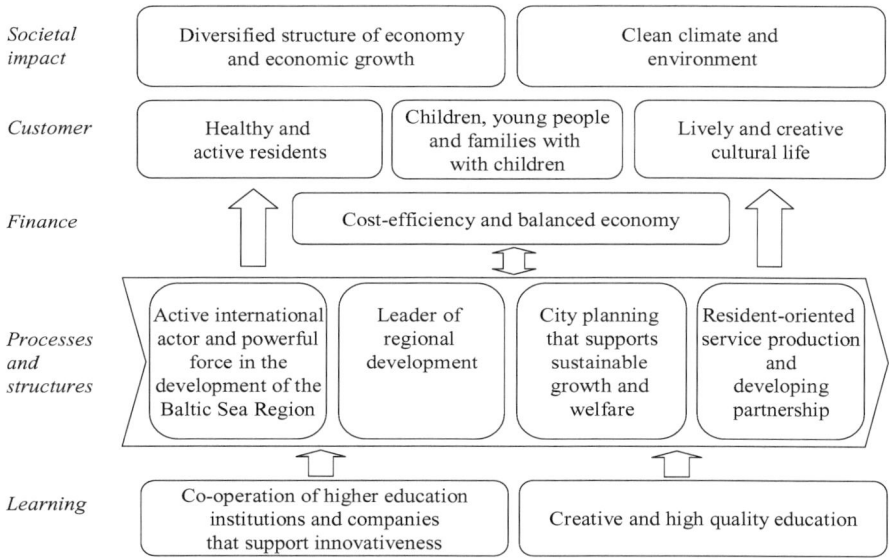

The strategic architecture

An outstanding city strategy is not a random collection of unit strategies but a carefully constructed system of interdependent plans. The elements of the strategies should be aligned with one another to create synergies. The alignment of the unit strategy is driven by the unit's environmental situation and, on the other hand, its operation in the city organization. This kind of alignment is also applied in large business companies (Collis and Montgomery, 1998). The city can create a significant strategic advantage by better integrating the strategic themes, objectives and measures of different units with the city-level strategic plan. It can create synergies through the integration of services provided for its residents. Such integration, however, typically cannot happen without the active role of management.

The City Board approved the strategic plan of the City of Turku in May 2005. Strategic objectives were defined for each strategic theme. The City Board approved the city-level Balanced Scorecard in June 2005 to implement the strategic plan. The measures and targets were set for the years 2006 and 2009. Responsibilities were laid upon the Mayor and Deputy Mayors to implement the strategic initiatives and achieve the city-level objectives. The Balanced Scorecard provides the framework to evaluate the progress made along with plans for new strategic initiatives. The executive management boards led by the Mayor and the sector management boards led by the Deputy Mayors use the scorecards and objectives for framing the discussion for major strategic initiatives.

An example of the objectives is that Turku will be an active international actor and a powerful force in the development of the Baltic Sea Region. The target of the city-level scorecard is that Turku should identify the networks and their contents by 2006. The desired target by 2009 is that the city will participate actively in the development processes of the area. In this way the City Council aims to increase its role in regional development, not only in its local region, but also in a larger international area. The Mayor is responsible for achieving this objective.

The City Board of Turku instructed all operating units to develop their strategies in line with the overall strategy. The City of Turku has four shared support units, 22 operating units and eight municipal companies. The administrative units defined their Balanced Scorecards during the budget process. The Balanced Scorecards have also been defined in most cases for the departments of the units. The activities of the administrative units are aligned and linked together to support the city-level strategy. These linkages establish the practice of managing the entire city as a single entity.

The Balanced Scorecard is a tool to integrate the objectives of the different units. The directors of the operating units have an active role in the strategy process of the City of Turku. They are responsible for leading the strategy process of their operative units. The process of planning the strategies and scorecards of the operating units enabled the units define their strategic themes and objectives to contribute both to the unit's performance and the city's strategic themes and objectives. An example is that the Turku University of Applied Sciences has an objective to expand international relations and student exchange supporting the citywide objective. Selected measures of operating units are approved annually by the City Council in the city budget.

4. The Balanced Scorecard integrated into budgeting

Budgeting as a process for implementing the strategy

Budgeting is the primary management process in most organizations, and is typically carried out separately from strategic planning (Kaplan and Norton, 2001). This is based on the traditional theoretical thinking that operational management is different from strategic management (Anthony, 1965). However, these two approaches can be integrated to complement each other.

The budget has traditionally helped managers primarily with the tactical processes. Managers review the operating performance against the budget and take corrective action if necessary during the budget year. Budgets are useful when the major issues are to control costs and implement a cost-efficiency strategy. If budgets are the primary means to exercise control in organizations the short-term financial targets win the primary management attention. The actions of management are directed at short-term operational details.

The budget should also allocate resources to the strategic initiatives to achieve long-term objectives. This kind of budgeting supports the focus strategy to create economic growth and welfare in the future. The organization can pursue a cost efficiency strategy but at the same time management takes actions to direct the resources to achieve the long-term strategic objectives. Management allocates resources to traditional investments, but an increasing amount of investments is made in human capital.

The existing budgeting process must be linked to the strategy, because the strategy is critical for organizational success in a knowledge economy. If resources are not directed toward achieving the strategic objectives, these will remain distant goals to which the organization is not committed. The advantage of the Balanced Scorecard is that the operating units can see how their objectives contribute to the city-level strategic objectives.

The strategic objectives that the organization must achieve should be set in the various perspectives and described using causal relationships. Resources and strategic initiatives are deployed to bridge the gap between current and stretch targets to be achieved. Short-term targets must be set for the values of the measures. Traditionally the budgeting process sets targets for financial measures, but the Balanced Scorecard expands the budgeting to incorporate targets from other perspectives.

The budgeting must identify the strategic initiatives, the units and individuals responsible for the implementation and timetable. The persons responsible must drill each programme down into one or more action plans and include these programmes in the operating budget. The monitoring of action plans and the budget will then become part of the periodic review process of management. The operational units of the City of Turku report on the achievement of measures three times a year.

The Balanced Scorecard of the operating units

An example is given of how the Balanced Scorecards are used in the operating units of the city. The Turku University of Applied Sciences is owned and maintained by the City of Turku and is one of city's operating units. The Turku University of Applied Sciences has six educational departments, a continuing education centre and ten shared support units. All of these administrative units have their own Balanced Scorecards, which directly contribute to the overall Balanced Scorecard of the institution.

Table 1 describes the Balanced Scorecard of the Turku University of Applied Sciences. It includes five perspectives including societal impact, customer, finance, processes and structures and learning, which have ten strategic objectives. The objectives include 37 measures, which have target values for the planning period 2006 - 2008. The scorecard also identifies 16 measures that are relevant to support the overall strategy of the City of Turku. The measures and targets are updated annually during the budget process in the internal target discussions. The column for 2005 includes actual figures. The targets for the planning period 2006 - 2008 were agreed in internal target discussions in the autumn 2005.

The societal impact has been measured by the share of graduates who find employment immediately after graduation. Another measure is the share of graduates who settle in Southwest Finland. Both of these measures and their target values have been considered so important that they are approved by the City Council and reviewed three times in a year. The share of entrepreneurs among graduates and the share of theses written for working life have targets approved by the Turku University of Applied Sciences.

Table 1. Balanced Scorecard of the Turku University of Applied Sciences

Perspectives and objectives	Measures	2005	2006	2007	2008
Societal impact:					
• Regional development	• Entrepreneurs of graduates, %	2	3	3.5	4
	• Employed graduates, % *	83	75	75	75
	• Graduates who remain in the region, % *	75	75	75	75
	• Share of theses written for working life, %	85	90	95	95
Customer:					
• Customer satisfaction	• Student satisfaction on a scale 1-5 where 5 is highest, young students *	3.3	3.4	3.4	3.4
	• Student satisfaction on a scale 1-5 where 5 is highest, adult students *	3.4	3.4	3.4	3.4
	• Employer satisfaction on a scale 1-5 where 5 is highest *	3.6	3.7	3.7	3.7
	• No. of applicants per study place *	4.4	4.8	4.8	4.8
Finance:					
• Funding from central government	• No. of graduates, young students *	1310	1320	1350	1380
	• No. of graduates, adult students *	200	210	220	240
• External funding	• External R&D income, 1000 €	3000	3100	3700	4500
	• External funding, 1000 €	4900	5100	7500	8000
	• External R&D income / total expenses, %	5	6	7	8
	• External funding / total expenses, % *	14.7	18	20	22
	• Service income, 1000 €	1000	1100	1300	1500
Processes and structures:					
• R&D	• No. of R&D projects	136	180	175	170
	• R&D expenses / total expenses, % *	7	8	9	10
	• No. of researchers / no. of teachers, %	13	13	16	19
	• No. of publications	75	75	75	75
• International relations	• No. of outgoing exchange students *	323	353	380	400
	• No. of incoming exchange student *	248	279	307	320
• Education	• No. of students in due period of study / no. of all students, % *	80	82	83	84
	• No. of students / no. of teachers	22	22	24	26
	• No. of degrees, young students, %	1337	1400	1450	1500
	• No. of degrees, adult students, %	200	210	220	260
	• Average length of study in years, young students, %	4.3	4.1	4	4
	• Average length of study in years, adult students, %	3.1	3.1	3	2.9
	• Average no. of credits, young students	50	50	54	58
	• Average no. of credits, adult students	50	51	52	54
	• Drop-outs among young students, % *	6.7	8	7	6
	• Drop-outs among adult students, % *	11	10	9	8
	• No. of credits in virtual learning	14000	15000	15000	16000
Learning:					
• R&D capabilities	• No. of licentiate degrees *	52	80	75	70
	• No. of doctorates *	42	50	60	70
• Education capabilities	• Share of teachers with teacher education, %	75	80	82	85

* The asterisk indicates the measures that directly contribute to the strategy of the City of Turku and are approved by the City Council.

The objective of customer satisfaction is measured by the attractiveness of the institution and by the number of applicants per study place. The aim is also to increase student and employer satisfaction and keep them at a reasonably high level. These measures are also approved annually by the City Council and regularly reviewed.

The financial perspective includes two measures that are approved by the City Council. The number of graduates is important, because the institution receives unit-priced funding from central government. Another measure approved by the City Council is the external funding as the share of the total expenses. The rest of the measures in the financial perspective are important to the Turku University of Applied Sciences but they are not approved by the City Council and are excluded from the city's budget book.

The processes and structures perspective includes measures describing the volume of R&D, student exchange and efficient study processes, which are approved by the City Council. These measures describe the educational process of the degree programmes. Many measures describing the study process are omitted from centrally approved objectives. The performance of these activities is measured only against the objectives of the Turku University of Applied Sciences.

The learning perspective includes the measures describing the capabilities of the personnel. The number of licentiate degrees and doctorates is approved for the targets by the City Council. Even though the other measures are important, the City Board cannot approve and follow every important aspect of service production in a large city organization. Otherwise it would be difficult to evaluate what the most important measures for the communication and implementation of the strategy are at the city level.

Management information system

When the Balanced Scorecard approach was introduced in 2002 at the Turku University of Applied Sciences, the existing information systems did not support the new approach. It was evident that without automation the collection of data and aggregation of the scorecards to the upper organizational levels was troublesome. The institution developed the management information system, which collects data from the various operational data sources to the data warehouse. The portal of the systems was planned to directly support the management process (Kettunen, 2004, 2005; Kettunen and Kantola, 2005).

The management information system was planned to increase strategic awareness and encourage innovations and development activities. The system includes communication, dialogue and collaboration, which are the essential features of any management process. The reciprocal open discussion about strategic objectives supports the commitment of the personnel to the strategic plans and continuous improvement. The persons at the different organizational levels use the portal as a platform to draft their strategies, budgets, action and human resource plans and reports. The members of the personnel have diverse user rights and roles in the portal.

In every hierarchical organization, with superior-subordinate-relationships, there is necessarily at least a certain degree of accountability. The management information system is not considered in our case to be judgment-oriented and accountability-driven. Rather, it has been emphasised that the action plan is essentially every manager's own plan to balance the different strategic objectives. The management information system should be seen as a self-evaluation and improvement-oriented tool, which is a platform to document the traits of strategic awareness, create the organizational memory and achieve the strategic objectives.

The manager is expected to evaluate the current state of affairs in the portal. Then the manager is expected to evaluate to which extent the unit has achieved the agreed strategic objectives using the classification: objectives achieved to the full extent, objectives partly achieved and objectives not achieved all. Based on the self-evaluation the manager is expected to identify the goals of development and the means to achieve the goals. In addition, the manager sets the timetables and identifies individuals responsible for the planned tasks.

The action plan is located in the management portal and it can be seen as a useful tool to collect and store information to the collective memory of the organization. Furthermore, by referring to the portal the institution can provide the external auditors of quality assurance system with evidence on the use of evaluation information in the management process and about development steps taken on the basis of recognised weaknesses. The experience achieved at the Turku University of Applied Sciences has encouraged the City of Turku to plan the system for the whole city organization.

5. Conclusions

The introduction of the Balanced Scorecard to an organization is a learning process. Organizations may delay the start, because they are not sure whether they have selected the right measures, or because data are not available for all the measures. The experience of the City of Turku shows that this is an iterative learning process. Every meeting brings some new elements and helps managers to define a balanced set of performance drivers and outcome indicators.

The scorecard stimulated an intense management dialogue and helped the managers and employees to better understand the existing strategy. From the viewpoint of managers the Balanced Scorecard helped the City of Turku to communicate its strategic objectives and implement the strategy. The process of building the scorecard has also been a mechanism for creating better strategic plans.

The Balanced Scorecard provides the workers in each department with a clear understanding of how their work contributes to citywide strategic objectives. The ownership of the objectives and measures give the responsibility to individuals and various administrative units. The Balanced Scorecard enables the evaluation and adjudication of the results. It is primarily a tool to see how different administrative units have succeeded in implementing their strategies.

The traditional budgeting of public organizations can be integrated with the strategy at the different levels of large organizations. The Balanced Scorecard extends traditional budgeting, helping the organizations to define their objectives, measures and targets in the planning period in various perspectives. The integration helps to direct the resources to achieve other strategic objectives. The linkages between the objectives in the different perspectives help the personnel and other stakeholders to understand the big picture of how the city works and how it can achieve the desired outcomes.

The Balanced Scorecard is a useful tool in large organizations. It is also a tool for the network of municipalities and other organizations to develop the region. The networks can define joint strategic themes that can be taken into account in the partners' strategies. Then joint and organization-specific objectives and measures can be defined for each cooperative organization. The Balanced

Scorecard approach can help the networks in the development of mutually interesting issues such as environment, culture and education.

The strategic and action plans with the measures of the Balanced Scorecard located in the management information system are useful tools to collect and store information to the collective memory of the organization and strengthen its strategic awareness. The collaborative and interactive use of the information system supports the organizational self-evaluation and helps management and employees to improve the action plans to achieve the strategic objectives. If the system was used only diagnostically as a monitoring device concentrating on the deviations from the target values without face-to-face interaction and negotiation the full potential of the system can not be achieved.

References

Anthony, R.N. (1965). *Management planning and control systems: A framework for analysis.* Boston: HBS Press.

Askim, J. (2004). Performance management and organizational intelligence: Adapting the Balanced Scorecard in Larvik Municipality. *International Public Management Journal, 7*(3), 415-438.

Collis, D., & Montgomery, C. (1998). Creating corporate advantage, *Harvard Business Review*, May-June, 70-83.

Davies, B., & Ellison, L. (2003). *The new strategic direction and development of the school.* London: Routledge Falmer.

Drucker, P. (1994). The theory of business. *Harvard Business Review*, September-October, 95-104.

Fidler, B. (2002). *Strategic management for school development.* London: Paul Chapman Publishing.

Frigo, M.L., & Krumwiede, K.R. (1999). Balanced Scorecard: A rising trend in strategic performance measurement. *Journal of Strategic Performance Measurement*, February-March, 42-48.

Jessop, B., & Sum, N.L. (2000). The entrepreneurial city in action: Hong Kong's emerging strategies in and for (inter)urban competition. *Urban Studies, 37*(12), 2287-2313.

Johnson, G., & Scholes, K. (2002). *Exploring corporate strategy: Text and cases.* Cambridge: Prentice Hall.

Joldersma, C., & Winter, V. (2002). Strategic management in hybrid organizations. *Public Management Review, 4*(1), 83-99.

Kaplan, R., & Norton, D. (1992). The Balanced Scorecard: Measures that drive performance. *Harvard Business Review*, January-February, 71-79.

Kaplan, R., & Norton, D. (1993). Putting the Balanced Scorecard to work. *Harvard Business Review*, September-October, 134-147.

Kaplan, R.S., & Norton, D.P. (1996). *The Balanced Scorecard.* Boston, MA: Harvard Business School Press.

Kaplan, R.S., & Norton, D.P. (2001). *The strategy-focused organization.* Boston, MA: Harvard Business School Press.

Kaplan, R.S., & Norton, D.P. (2004). *Strategy maps.* Boston, MA: Harvard Business School Press.

Kettunen, J. (2002). Competitive strategies in higher education, *Journal of Institutional Research, 11*(2), 38-47.

Kettunen, J. (2003). Strategic evaluation of institutions by students in higher education. *Perspectives: Policy and Practice in Higher Education, 7*(1), 14-18.

Kettunen, J. (2004). The strategic evaluation of regional development in higher education. *Assessment and Evaluation in Higher Education, 29*(3), 357-368.

Kettunen, J. (2005). Implementation of strategies in continuing education. *The International Journal of Educational Management, 19*(3), 207-217.

Kettunen, J., & Kantola, I. (2005). Management information system based on the Balanced Scorecard. *Campus-Wide Information Systems, 22*(5), 263-274.

Lingle, J.H., & Shieman, W.A. (1996). From Balanced Scorecards to strategic gauges: Is measurement worth it? *Management Review*, March, 56-62.

Nonaka, I., & Takeuchi, H. (1995). *The knowledge-creating company.* New York: Oxford University Press.

Porter, M. (1990). *The competitive advantage of nations.* London: Macmillan.

Porter, M. (1996). What is strategy? *Harvard Business Review*, November-December, 61-78.

Rucci, A.J., Kirn, S.P., & Quinn, R.T. (1998). The Employee-customer-profit chain at Sears. *Harvard Business Review*, January-February, 82-97.

Schein, E.H. (1985). *Organizational culture and leadership.* San Francisco: Jossey Bass.

Steiss, A.W. (2003). *Strategic management for public and nonprofit organisations.* New York: Marcel Dekker.

Takeuchi, H., & Nonaka, I. (2004). *Hitotsubashi on knowledge management.* Singapore: John Wiley & Sons.

Treacy, M., & Wiersema, F. (1995). *The discipline of market leaders: Choose your customers, narrow your focus, dominate your market.* Reading, MA: Addison-Wesley.

Wheelen, T.L., & Hunger, J.D. (1995). *Strategic management and business policy*. Reading, MA: Addison-Wesley.

VII. Competitive Strategies in Higher Education

1. Introduction

The role of heads of departments has attracted the attention of educational researchers only comparatively recently (e.g. Floyd and Wooldridge, 1996, Gold, 1998). However, reference to the importance of involving heads of departments and other staff in key decisions is frequently noted (e.g. Dearing, 1994). This chapter is a theoretical analysis about strategic management and makes a contribution to the literature by focusing on the heads of departments and competitive strategies of subunits in higher education.

The strategy process means the manner and style in which teaching, management and support processes are planned for a better future. Many heads of departments are usually involved in helping to shape the strategic plans of educational institutions, primarily by commenting on drafts of the whole institutional plan. Their role can, however, be much larger, because they are responsible for developing their own departmental plan with their staff.

One key choice in strategic planning is the decision whether the central plan is created and translated into more localised planning in departments or whether strategic planning is an amalgam of subunit development plans. The central plan cannot be a collection of separate plans produced by subunits. There is a need for a whole-organisational approach, which gives general broad lines and which is mediated by, for example, the approving board of governors. There is also a need to create ownership and give content to the central plan by allowing subunits to contribute their own strategic aims to the central plan.

The broad lines of the central plan provide the basis for the subunit strategic plans. It is emphasised in this study that the central plan should be broad enough to allow subunits to develop their own competitive strategies. These strategies of subunits can be highly different from each other depending the public control, funding regulations and other constraints. If the central plan and environmental changes are taken into account, the plans produced by subunits usually need only minor modifications.

Michael Porter (1990) has introduced three potentially successful competitive strategies, which are the overall cost leadership, differentiation and focus. The aim of this study is to explore how the competitive strategies known in the business literature can be applied to market-oriented educational institutions. These generic strategies provide an interesting basis for the strategic management of subunits in higher education institutions.

Higher education institutions face competition from universities, polytechnics, private training companies and consultants. They must respond to the complex factors making an impact on the demand for education. At the same time, they are constrained by state control of the methods in which they may operate. Their strategies are, therefore, planned in an environment, which is a hybrid of commercial and public sector constituents.

Heads of departments often have very little time for strategic thinking and planning, either within their department, or across the school as a whole (Earley and Fletcher-Campbell, 1992). Heads of departments may spend much of their time teaching, routine administration and crisis management. The effective head of department is able to think strategically about what is in the best long-term interest for the future of the subunit and the organisation as a whole.

This chapter is organised as follows: The strategic approach to the management of higher education institutions is analysed in Section 2. Especially the role of heads of departments is discussed. The competitive strategies are presented in Section 3. The primary emphasis is in the market-led continuing education. Finally, the results of the study are summarized and discussed in the concluding section.

2. Strategic management

Strategic management can be seen a matter of essential economic analysis and planning. It can also be seen as a matter of organisational decision making within a social, political and cultural process (Johnson and Scholes, 1993). Strategic management involves taking a view of the whole organisation, its place in its environment, its values and culture, its key purpose, its direction and its strategic choice for the better future. Strategic management is a matter of bridge building or mapping the route between the perceived present situation and the desired future situation (West-Burnham, 1994).

The strategic approach to management allows the heads of educational institutions to develop their organisations holistically and to integrate curriculum, staff, finance and external relations. Strategic planning is a continuous process in administration which links goal-setting, policy-making, short-term and long-term planning, budgeting and spans all levels of the organisation. The rapid pace of change means that strategy is an evolving, ongoing and uncertain process.

There is much in written business literature, which is not relevant for education. Educational institutions are not in an open market, where they are free to change course, according to any sudden environmental changes or, close down and begin again. However, there is a part of business literature, which is relevant to education, and it does seem that there are elements of the business approach to planning that are relevant in higher education. Porter's (1990) concepts of competitive strategies can be successfully applied to the educational environment.

There is likely to be a range of constraints imposed by national government, local stakeholders or the competitiveness from neighbouring institutions. These include the imposition of financial regimes, which relate to the ambiguous position of educational institutions in operating within the public sector in a competitive business environment.

The external imperatives have to be taken into account, when developing a plan, and decisions have to be made regarding the external factors which are most important for the particular institutional context. These constraints may be highly variable in different subunits of educational institutions. Therefore, a specific competitive strategy reflecting its particular circumstances is required for each subunit.

The strategic planning covers usually a timescale of three to five years. Any shorter-term development planning is produced from the strategic plan, relating to the timescale of approximately one year. These shorter-term plans include targets and performance indicators, and indicate the details of a specific action. Heads of departments are in a key position to implement strategies.

Self-management and accountability

Over recent years there has been a shift in many countries to greater autonomy and self-management of schools, colleges and higher education institutions. Examples can be found in Australia, England and Wales, Hong Kong, Israel, New Zealand and the USA (Bush and Coleman, 2000). Central governments have put great pressure on educational leaders to inspire their staff towards improvement.

Caldwell and Spinks (1992) show that self-management is underpinned by the following assumptions:
• Managers will be more responsive to their clients if they are able to determine the nature and quality of education.
• Managers will be able to determine the precise mix of resources allocated to the education in order to achieve the objectives.
• Staff will have the incentive to maximise efficiency in the use of resources in order to use the savings to enhance the quality of education further.
• Standards will rise as clients articulate their needs and educational institutions respond to these needs, to satisfy the enrolled students and attract new.

The international trend of education systems towards greater autonomy and self-governance has changed the demands for those who assume the responsibility to manage the institutions. Choices have to be made at a national level regarding the broad lines of educational policy, but an increasing number of decisions have to be made at the institutional level.

Higher education institutions have found themselves in the position of undertaking planning which will determine the institution's continued survival and development in a highly competitive environment. Institutions have been left with the task of interpreting external requirements rather than determining directly the aims of institutions.

The greater autonomy for educational institutions has been accompanied by a significantly increased market orientation. Education is moving from a public service driven by professionals to a market-driven service, fuelled by customers. Strategic management requires the ability to integrate different aspects of the educational institution to ensure the best possible economic and educational outcomes.

Higher education institutions have to recognize the accountability of their plans and implementation, because they are bounded by legislation, public control and financing. Even though their income may be crucial, the public service is not only for competitive advantage but also for specific educational purposes.

Accountability means that higher education institutions operate within defined purposes, strategies and visions for the future to satisfy the demands of public control. Further, heads of departments are accountable for their strategic plans to senior management and the public control, but much depends upon the nature and quality of internal strategic management at the subunit level.

The role of heads of departments

This part of the study analyses the role of heads of departments in matters of strategy and strategic management. It is emphasised that strategic management of heads of departments can be crucial for organisational success. This is important, if the educational and business environments of departments are different from each other. Especially in larger organisations, a greater degree of responsibility has been devoted to subunits.

Floyd and Wooldridge (1996) emphasise the importance of middle management in formulation and implementation of strategies. They point out that the strategic roles of middle managers are to champion innovative initiatives, facilitate adaptability to new behaviour, synthesise information within and outside the organisation and implement strategy. Middle managers include administrative managers, who also have an input to make in strategic management.

Heads of departments are curriculum and programme managers, who have a major responsibility for the planning and implementation of organisational aims and objectives as expressed in strategic plans. Leaders need assistants who can articulate the results in practical terms and work with their colleagues to turn the strategy into reality. Heads of departments have also an important role in passing information and ideas from the front line to organisational leaders.

Heads of departments are likely to be perceived by organisational leaders as an important source of information concerning the external world and its likely impact on their areas of responsibility or expertise. Managers have responsibility for the work of other adults and their activities such as planning, organising, resourcing, controlling, evaluating and leading. They have an important role in strategic planning and decision-making at both subunit and central level.

Heads of departments can be criticised by senior staff for their rather limited or subject-bound perspectives. These views may, however, be regarded as an advantage for the organisation, but on the other hand, the subject-bound thoughts and competitive strategies of subunits should not be in contradiction with the strategy of the whole organisation.

Involvement of subunits in strategic matters is likely to vary according to the nature of education, type of customers, funding bodies and regulations. It is also likely to vary according to the nature and culture of the organisation. A key question is whether the subunits are expected or encouraged to be involved in strategy formulation and link the strategy to subunits' external environment?

According to Peters (1988) the essence of strategy is the creation of organisational capabilities that will allow the persons to react opportunistically to whatever happens. In the fully developed organisation, the front line person should also be capable of being involved in strategy making. All teachers and planners in higher education are managers in that they are responsible for the management of students, the management of the learning process and resources.

An organisation is developed to achieve certain goals of objectives by group activity (Cyert, 1975). In the strategy process all the members of the organisation should envision its future and develop the necessary procedures to achieve that future. It can be emphasised that heads of departments have an important role in the formulating the strategy of a subunit with all its members in order to reach the educational objectives, increase its competitive advantage and also the well-being of the whole organisation.

The evaluation of strategies

Strategic evaluation may be used at the formulation stage to judge the merits of particular strategic alternatives. Johnson and Scholes (1993) suggest the strategic evaluation criteria of suitability, feasibility and acceptability as benchmarks against which organisations might judge the merits of particular strategies. The evaluation of strategic options requires sensible judgements on how these requirements should be weighed against each other.

Suitability is a criterion for assessing the extent to which a proposed strategy is consistent with the environment in which it is operating. A series of questions can be raised to evaluate the strategic options. Does the strategy exploit the strengths of the subunit and whole organisation? How far does the strategy overcome the difficulties identified in the strategic analysis? How well are the strategies of subunits in line with the strategy of the whole organisation? Does the strategy adopted fit in with the main purpose of the organisation?

Feasibility is a criterion for assessing whether the strategy can be implemented successfully. Can the necessary market position be achieved? Can the strategy be funded? Are the subunits and organisation capable of performing the required level? Will the reactions of heads of departments, staff and students be manageable? How will the organisation ensure that the required knowledge and skills are available in each subunit of the organisation?

The *acceptability* criterion is related to internal and external relationships. The key question to be considered is, how acceptable are the strategies of subunits to each other and the overall strategy? Will the strategy match the expectations of students, teachers, managers and senior staff? Another key question is related to the expectations of stakeholders. Each stakeholder who is concerned about the activities and performance of the educational institution has its own set of criteria to determine how well the organisation is performing.

Strategic evaluation using the criteria of suitability, feasibility and acceptability emphasise the need to formulate different strategies for subunits. The strategic analysis of subunits, which operate in their specific environments, lead to different kinds of strategic choices. The capabilities, knowledge and skills may be highly variable across the subunits, and therefore, different kinds of steps can be taken in the future. Furthermore, the expectations of stakeholders emphasise the need to define specific strategies for the subunits.

3. Generic competitive strategies

This section describes the generic strategies presented by Porter (1990) and explores how heads of departments can use them to define the strategies of departments. It turns out that the competitive strategies of companies can be successfully used in higher education institutions, particularly in continuing education centres, which operate in a market-led environment.

The best strategy of an organisation is ultimately a unique construction, which reflects its particular circumstances. Porter has presented three internally consistent generic strategies, which can be used singly or in combination to create a strong position in the long run. The three strategies are overall cost leadership, differentiation and focus. The three generic strategies are alternative approaches to dealing with the competitive markets.

The organisation failing to develop its strategy, in at least one of the three directions, is in an extremely poor strategic situation. Such an organisation is almost guaranteed low profitability and quality. The organisation stuck in this position should make a fundamental decision to develop its strategy. An organisation stuck in the middle of competitive strategies must either take steps to achieve cost effectiveness or at least cost parity, which involves aggressive measures to develop the process. Alternatively, it must differentiate itself to achieve some uniqueness. The third strategy is to focus itself on a particular target market.

Effectively implementing any of these strategies requires total commitment and supporting arrangements. A large organisation can, however, have more than one primary target in its departments or subunits and pursue more than one approach, if there are different environments, competitive situations and supporting organisational arrangements in these subunits.

Overall cost leadership

The strategy of overall cost leadership is achieved through a set of functional policies aimed at this basic objective. Cost leadership requires the construction of efficient-scale facilities and a vigorous pursuit of cost reductions in areas such as research and development, service and marketing. A great deal of managerial attention is necessary in order to achieve cost efficiency.

A low-cost position provides substantial entry barriers in terms of cost advantages or scale economies. A low-cost position defends the organisation against powerful buyers. A strategy of overall cost leadership is an appropriate choice in markets where the price level is relatively low defined by the public sector funding bodies or due to a hard competition in the market. Low cost also provides a defence against input cost increases. Achieving a low overall cost position often requires favourable access to input.

The general objective of a higher education institution is to promote its students' learning within a curriculum, which is suitable to the environment, feasible to the organisation and acceptable to its stakeholders. An educational institution should meet these ends efficiently and effectively. In such an organization tensions will arise between the professional autonomy and managerial control. The head of the educational institution and heads of departments have the dual roles of a leading professional and chief executive.

The terminology is not always clear and consistently used. According to Simkins (1998) efficiency means the achievement of given outcomes at least cost and effectiveness means the matching of results with objectives. Efficiency and effectiveness require that academic managers in higher education institutions should be aware of the full cost of the activities.

Efficiency is defined in an educational context as property, which makes good use of all its available resources to achieve the best possible educational outcomes for all its students and in doing so provides excellent value for money. The concept of effectiveness is often used among the key performance indicators.

The centrally driven funding mechanism which emphasises the management of inputs encourages institutions to develop resource management strategies based on efficiency, but on the other hand, the mechanism which emphasises the outcome leads to performance based on effectiveness. The findings of earlier studies of schools suggest that losers are more likely to concentrate on efficiency strategies. On the other hand, winners use effectiveness strategies. The winners also use the opportunity to increase the resources (Simkins, 1994). Much seems to depend on the style of management.

The Open University in Finland is able to derive benefits from the favourable access to input, because it uses the faculty teachers. They are able to teach the same course at the Open University, as in the department of the faculty with relatively low costs. A low overall cost position may well require designing products easy to produce. The arrangement of joint courses by the Open University with the department of the faculty is one way to reach this requirement efficiently.

The position of low overall costs is achieved in the labour market training of Finnish continuing education centres by their own teaching staff. Own teaching staff is used, because faculty teachers are typically not available. The management of visiting teachers brings costs and they are usually more expensive compared to own staff. This may require maintaining a wide line of related courses to spread costs and serve all the major customer groups to build sufficient volume. Once achieved, the high margins of the low-cost position can be reinvested in new equipment, facilities and knowledge to maintain cost leadership.

A low-cost education does not mean developing programmes which are significantly better than others. The target is not to provide the highest quality, but to produce a low-cost product, which has sufficient quality. A low-cost strategy means to develop an educational product that is truly simple to produce and has a low price and finally a high market share.

Differentiation

The differentiation strategy is achieved creating something perceived as being unique in educational markets. An organisation may differentiate itself within several dimensions. Differentiation can be achieved by brand image, technology, customer service or other dimensions. The differentiation strategy does not allow ignoring costs, but rather they are not the primary strategic target.

Differentiation is a viable strategy for earning above-average returns, because it creates a defensible position for coping with competitive forces. Differentiation yields higher margins, since brand loyal buyers lack comparable alternatives and are thereby less price sensitive. The customer loyalty and uniqueness provide entry barriers for the competitors, because the organisation is better positioned against substitutes than its competitors.

Differentiation is a viable strategy in educational markets, because the objective of many institutions is the brand loyalty by customers. This is especially true in market-led continuing education, but there are also brands in public funded education. A degree is an educational brand. A highly recognised degree motivates students in effective learning. Students aiming for a degree, are not likely to select courses that cannot be included in the programme.

An educational programme following the differentiation strategy may have a prestigious title such as Master of Business Administration (MBA), it may have extremely high-quality courses abroad, the best lecturers and good care of customers, all of which are crucial in attracting high-income business managers to this expensive education (Kettunen, 1999, 2000). Differentiation requires a perception of exclusivity.

There are many Master's programmes, which may follow the differentiation strategy. A Master of Quality, Master of Security, Master of Social Work and Health Care and many others provide attractive titles. Exclusivity is reached within executive management education and conferences by carefully selecting the participants or using world-famous academics and other outstanding persons within their field to give their presentations.

Students nationwide acknowledge the superiority of the differentiated education, which is based on extensive research, educational planning, high quality teaching and intensive student support. It also requires strong marketing abilities, reputation for quality, a long tradition and amenities to attract highly skilled labour, scientists and creative people. However, not all customers are willing or able to pay the required higher fees.

Focus

The strategy of focusing on a particular customer group or segment of the product line may take several kinds of forms. The focus can be on a geographic market, an occupational group, at organisational level or a type of education. The functional policy is developed to serve a particular target very well. It is assumed that it is possible to serve the narrow strategic target more efficiently or effectively than other organisations which are operating more broadly.

Even though the focus strategy does not aim to achieve low costs or differentiation, it does achieve one or both of these positions. As a result of the focus strategy the organisation achieves lower costs, because of low-cost production or its distribution system. Alternatively, the organisation is better able to meet the specialised needs of the particular customer. The focus strategy implies limitations on the over-all market share achievable, because it involves a trade-off between profitability and sales volume.

The focus strategy may mean reducing the customer list to the main leading customers or chains. The focus strategy approaches the concept of collaboration. Cardno (1990) defines collaboration as a term employed to express partnership, cooperation, agreement, consent and working in combination to accomplish institutional objectives.

A close collaboration with one specific customer is an extreme form of focus strategy. Some educational institutions in Finland, for example, Jollas Instituutti and K-instituutti, serve only certain large retail companies. The focus strategy implies limitations on the over-all market share achievable, but involves trade-off between profitability and sales volume.

A specific form of focus strategy is to serve certain occupational groups. For example, The Educational Unit of Vantaa Institute for Continuing Education, which belongs to the University of Helsinki, has for a long time focused on the continuing education of teachers and principals of primary and secondary schools. It has reduced its customer list mainly to the city of Vantaa and other municipalities in the neighbourhood.

Occupation-specific training is predominant at the continuing education centres of Finnish polytechnics. Typically the basic education at polytechnics are occupation oriented compared to the subject-oriented training at universities. Therefore the strategy of focus applied to occupations is a natural choice at the polytechnics.

4. Conclusions

A key challenge for those who are responsible for managing higher education institutions is the development of approaches to strategic management both at whole institution and subunit levels. The educational objectives should lead the process of strategic management, which ensures these purposes and not the other way round. The overall strategy should be broad enough to allow the definition of different competitive strategies for subunits to meet the different educational objectives.

Heads of departments have also an important role to offer advice, information and intelligence and thereby to think strategically for the future of the whole organisation. They are expected to think and act strategically in their own areas of responsibility. This is particularly important if the educational and business environment is different for the departments of the educational institution.

The higher education institutions which define their strategy predominantly in terms of senior management responsibilities at the top level of the organisation are unlikely to be making the best outcomes. It is important to encourage heads of departments and their staff to participate in their own strategy process in order to find out their competitive strategy, which is in line with the strategy of the institution as a whole.

It turns out that the three generic competitive strategies can be applied in the subunits of higher education institutions. This is especially true in the competitive markets of continuing education. The strategies of overall cost leadership, differentiation and focus, which have been presented in business literature, provide a good basis for the strategic management of subunits.

Typical examples of overall cost leadership are the Open University and the labour market training, which have generally low fees defined by funding bodies. Management education and degree-level education at university follow the strategy of differentiation. Focus strategy is applied in educational institutions which serve only certain chains of companies or organisations. It is also applied in continuing education which is targeted to certain occupations and geographical areas.

References

Bush, T. and M. Coleman (2000), Leadership and Strategic Management in Education, Paul Chapman Publishing Ltd, London.

Caldwell, B. and J. Spinks (1992), Leading the Self-Managing School, Falmer Press.

Cardno, C. (1990), Collaborative Management in New Zealand Schools, Auckland, Longman Paul.

Cyert, R. (1975), The Management of Non-Profit Organizations, Lexington, MA, Lexington Books.

Dearing, R. (1994), Strategic Planning in FE: The Impact of Incorporation, Blagdon, The Staff College.

Earley, P. and F. Fletcher-Campbell (1992), The Time to Manage? Department and Faculty Heads at Work, London, Routledge.

Floyd, S. and B. Wooldridge (1996), The Strategic Middle Manager, New York, Jossey-Bass.

Gold, A. (1998), Principles in Practice: Head of Department, London, Cassell.

Johnson, G. and K. Scholes (1993), Exploring Corporate Strategy, Hemel Hempstead, Prentice-Hall.

Kettunen, J. (1999), Customer Recommendations for MBA Programmes, International Journal: Continuous Improvement Monitor 4, 1-13.

Kettunen, J. (2000), Management Education and Organization Development, Reforms and Policy, In S. Tøsse, P. Falkencrone, A. Puurula and B. Bergstedt (eds.), Adult Education Research in Nordic Countries, Trondheim, Tapir Academic Press, 143-159.

Peters, T. (1988), Thriving on Chaos: A Handbook for Management Revolution, London, Macmillan.

Porter, M.E. (1990), The Competitive Advantage of Nations, London, Macmillan.

Simkins, T. (1994), Efficiency, Effectiveness and the Local Management of Schools, Journal of Education Policy 9, 15-33.

Simkins, T. (1998), Autonomy, Constraint and the Strategic Management of Resources, In D. Middlewood and J. Lumby (eds.), Strategic Management in Schools and Colleges, London, Paul Chapman Publishing Ltd.

West-Burnham, J. (1994), Strategy, Policy and Planning, In T. Bush and J. West-Burnham (eds.), The Principles of Educational Management, Harlow, Longman.

VIII. Implementation of Strategies in Continuing Education

1. Introduction

As the environment changes and learning takes place organisations refine and adapt their strategies. The evolution leads the organisation to a new strategy, which will be tested in real time. The organisation may learn that the new strategy is not working, because the senior managers only ask their people to aim at better results or customer satisfaction. This chapter provides the higher education institutions (HEI) with the strategies of continuing education and means to articulate, communicate and implement the strategy. It also demonstrates how these have been applied in continuing education.

Strategic management is a matter of bridge building between the perceived present situation and the desired future situation (Wheale, 1991 and West-Burnham, 1994). Strategy implies the movement of an organisation from its present position, described by the mission, to a desirable but uncertain future position, described by the vision. The Balanced Scorecard developed by Kaplan and Norton (1992, 1993) describes the strategy and strategic hypotheses using a set of explicit and testable cause-and-effect relationships.

The Balanced Scorecard creates and describes a holistic and measurable model of the organisation's strategy linked to the vision of the future. It helps to create a shared understanding about the efforts and needed steps for change. The Balanced Scorecard translates an organisation's strategy into tangible objectives and measures and balances them into four different perspectives: customers, financial outcomes, internal processes and learning.

The Balanced Scorecard is a general framework for describing and implementing strategy. Managers can use the Balanced Scorecard to communicate and educate the organisation about its strategy. The scorecard translates the strategy into linked cause-and-effect objectives and measures, which can be used to communicate the strategy to organisational subunits and workers.

Balanced Scorecards have been developed for business companies, but they are also applicable in public organisations. The Balanced Scorecards of HEIs look remarkably similar to those developed for profit-seeking corporations. They do not pay as much attention to the financial perspective, but emphasise more the role of customers and employees.

The empirical part of this chapter presents examples of the strategies for continuing education at Turku Polytechnic. It presents how the strategic themes, objectives and the linkages between the objectives can be described in a graphical representation. It also presents how the strategy of continuing education can be described with a numerical Balanced Scorecard including objectives, measures and targets for the planning period.

This chapter is organised as follows: Section 2 presents strategies for continuing education. Section 3 presents the Balanced Scorecards approach to implement the strategies effectively. Section 4 and 5 present examples of how the strategies can be described with strategy maps and Balanced Scorecards. Finally, the results of the study are summarized and discussed in the concluding section.

2. Strategies for continuing education

The value proposition describes a unique mix of product, service, relationship and image that the organisation provides for its customers. According to Porter (1990, 1996) there are three competitive strategies (see also Treacy and Wiersema, 1995 and Kettunen, 2002, 2003a). These strategies can also be applied in educational institutions.

1. Differentiation. A product leadership organisation pushes its products into the realm of the unknown, the untried or highly desirable.

2. Cost efficiency. Operationally excellent organisations deliver a combination of price and quality that creates competitive advantage.

3. Focus. A customer-intimate organisation builds bonds with its customers. It knows the people it sells to and the products and services they need. The focus strategy can be combined with differentiation and cost leadership.

The strategy of differentiation can be achieved by brand image, technology, customer service or other dimensions. Product leadership organisations can create something perceived to be unique. Differentiation requires a perception of exclusivity. Exclusivity is reached within executive management education and conferences by carefully selecting the participants or using world-famous academics and other outstanding individuals within their field to give their presentations.

A highly respected education motivates students to apply to the HEI. Students nationwide acknowledge the superiority of the differentiated education, which may be based on extensive research, educational planning, high-quality teaching and intensive support for students. It also requires good marketing abilities, a reputation for quality, a long tradition and features to attract highly skilled labour, scientists and creative people. Only relatively few customers are willing or able to pay the required higher fees of differentiated education.

A degree is an educational brand. An educational programme following the differentiation strategy may have a prestigious title such as the executive Master of Business Administration (eMBA), it may have extremely high-quality courses abroad, the best lecturers and good customer care, all of which are crucial in attracting high-income business managers to this expensive education (Kettunen, 2003b). There are many Master's programmes which may follow the differentiation strategy. Master of Quality, Master of Security, Master of Social Work and Health Care and many others provide attractive titles.

The strategy of cost efficiency emphasises measures of the cost reduction, economic efficiency, sufficient quality, and cycle time of internal processes. Perhaps the simplest and clearest objective is to reduce the unit cost of performing output. For sustain-stage educational institutions a target for keeping the costs in balance with revenue may be sufficient.

The productivity strategies focus on profitability by efficiency and cost reduction. The productivity strategy aims to improve cost structure and asset utilisation when serving the existing customer. One way to improve cost structure is to lower the costs of education and other services, and share common resources with other educational units.

Cost efficiency is a natural choice for strategy in the public sector, where financial resources are limited. The primary management and measurement should emphasise cost reduction and efficiency. Typically taxpayers provide the financial resources for educational institutions, which have limited annual budgets for their degree programmes. The position of low overall costs is also achieved in labour market training and in the Open University.

The strategy of focusing on a particular customer group or segment of the product line may take several different forms. The focus may be on a geographic market, an occupational group and an organisational level. The functional policy is developed to serve a particular target very well. Even though the focus strategy does not aim to achieve low costs or differentiation, it does achieve one or both of these positions.

Turku Polytechnic selected the strategy of focus for its overall strategy. It enables a customer-intimate education, which provides an excellent combination of costs and quality in education. The education is targeted at the region of Southwest Finland and also at its main clusters. Another feature of Finnish polytechnics is that the education is occupation specific. The strategy of focus was combined with the strategy of cost efficiency. An obvious reason for cost efficiency is that each educational programme has unit-priced funding provided by the government.

The strategy of focus can be adjusted *to the strategies of growth and profitability* according to where the strategic unit is in its life cycle. The starting phase often underlines the importance of the growth, but the mature phase emphasises the profitability. There is a trade-off between growth and productivity. The growth strategy highlights the opportunities for enhancing financial performance through revenue growth. The profitability strategy generally yields financial results sooner than the growth strategy.

The revenue growth strategy usually focuses on developing new products and services for existing customers or finding new customers for existing products. Very seldom are new products and services developed for new customers, because this requires vast amounts of new knowledge about new products, services and customers and a long time for development.

In their early-stage start-up continuing education centres see opportunities for rapid growth and emphasise objectives and measures to support this strategy. They typically enhance profitability strategy at the mature end of their life cycle. The continuing education centres that are in the middle of their life cycle define a "profitable growth" strategy that balances productivity and revenue growth. Profitable growth was selected for the strategy of the continuing education centre at Turku Polytechnic.

3. Balanced Scorecard translates the strategy into action

The measurements should be selected to correspond the strategy. If the growth strategy is selected the measures should be selected to describe the number of students, number of credits (ECTs) or any other measure describing how extensive the activities are. If the productivity strategy is selected the measures should describe the output produced in relation to the needed input or any measures which describe the productivity or profitability of the activities.

Usually the strategies of non-profit organisations in the public sector feature an operations excellence theme. Public sector organisations take their mission as given and try to reduce their costs, increase quality, and do it more efficiently. The non-profit organisations may, however, build competitive advantage in ways other than pure operational excellence.

The objective for growth-stage educational institutions is to focus on revenue enhancement. Educational institutions may choose financial objectives resulting from new products, customers, relationships, product and service mix and pricing. The educational institutions also choose objectives, which are the drivers of costs so that they keep the revenues and costs in balance.

The Balanced Scorecard was developed to provide a framework for the implementation of the strategy. The scorecard translates strategy into objectives and measures that can be communicated to the staff and external stakeholders. The Balanced Scorecard works best when it is used to communicate strategy and vision to inspire employees to find innovative ways to help the organisation succeed.

The implementation of the strategy is balanced between the external measures for customers, the measures of finance resulting from past efforts, the measures of internal processes, and the learning measures that drive future performance. These perspectives have been found to be necessary, sufficient and robust across a wide variety of organisations (Kaplan and Norton, 1996, 2001).

The results of the study by Lingle and Shieman (1996) show that measurement-managed companies tend to have better teamwork at the top, better communication throughout the organisation and better self-management at the bottom level. A survey by Frigio and Krumwiede (1999) concluded that the performance management systems which used Balanced Scorecard were significantly more effective compared to other systems.

The Balanced Scorecard approach is applied in many universities, for example, the University of Southern California and RMIT University (O'Neil et al., 1999). The method is widely used in Finnish universities. It is used, for example, at the University of Vaasa and Turku School of Economics and Business Administration. It is also widely used in Finnish polytechnics. For example, Turku Polytechnic, Tampere Polytechnic and Jyväskylä Polytechnic have used the approach.

The Balanced Scorecard translates the strategy into measurements. The main principle to link the scorecard to the strategy is to use cause-and-effect relationships between the perspectives. The measurement system should indicate the strategy through a sequence of relationships between performance drivers (leading indicators) and outcome measures (lagging indicators).

Performance drivers communicate how the outcomes can be achieved and provide an early indication of whether the strategy is being successfully implemented. There must be a strong linkage between the internal processes and financial measures. Economic efficiency is required for sufficient funding, but on the other hand funding is a precondition for internal processes.

A good measurement system should have a balanced mix of performance drivers and outcome measures that have been customised to the strategy. Organisations may also use diagnostic measures that monitor whether the processes remain under control. Diagnostic measures can be used to offset the temptation to achieve excellent performance in undesirable ways (Simons, 1995).

The best scorecards indicate the strategy so well that the strategy can be inferred by the collection of objectives and measures and the cause-and-effect relationships among them (Kaplan and Norton,

1996). Usually companies can formulate and communicate their strategy using approximately two dozen measurements. The exact number of measures is irrelevant because it depends on how many strategic measures are needed to describe and communicate the strategy and avoid sub-optimisation on any single measure.

4. Strategic themes and strategy maps

The strategy is a hypothesis of how the vision will be achieved. The strategic themes reflect what management believes must be done to succeed and to achieve strategic outcomes. Strategic themes are linked with the performance drivers and outcome measures. Each organisation has a unique set of strategic themes for producing results and creating value for customers.

Turku Polytechnic follows a customer-based strategy of focus by selecting an interrelated set of strategic themes to create distinct value for its students, their potential employers and the region. It has built its strategy around the main strategic statement of high quality learning and four strategic themes as follows:

Strategy of high quality learning
• *Turku Polytechnic will develop its region and reacts to the changes in its environment.*
• *Focus areas include biotechnology, information and communication technology, metal and maritime technology.*
• *Results of research and development will be used in education.*
• *Quality systems, assessment and in-house training will be used to develop the internal processes.*

The graphical representation of strategy on strategy maps provides a logical and comprehensive way to describe the organisation and its strategy. The strategy map clearly communicates the organisation's desired outcomes and how these outcomes can be achieved. It is the basis for the measurement system and enables the subunits of the organisation and employees to understand and implement the strategy.

Strategy maps provide tools to translate strategic statements into strategic themes, objectives, measures and targets. Strategy maps help the organisations see their strategies and detailed strategic themes in a graphical representation in an integrated and systematic way. They also help the staff to understand why specific targets have been set.

Figure 1 presents the strategy map of Turku Polytechnic. The process of drawing the strategy map and the linkages between the perspectives and objectives generated extensive thinking to reach a consensus about the functioning of the organisation, the role of strategic themes and how to implement the strategy effectively.

The strategy map describes the causal chains between the objectives. The customer perspective contains two objectives, which are "regional development" and "customer satisfaction". These objectives can be achieved by the innovation, support and learning processes described in the internal processes perspective.

The financial perspective includes the "external funding" and the "funding from central government". The external funding is used mainly to finance the innovation and support processes. The funding from central government is used to finance the support and learning processes. On the other hand, efficient processes enable sufficient funding.

The internal processes perspective includes a description of the sequential processes including research and development, support activities and education which form the causal chain of value creation. The objectives in the financial, and learning and growth perspectives have to be reached with the objectives in the internal processes to achieve the desired outcomes in regional development and customer satisfaction.

The learning and growth perspective includes three objectives: "the capability for R&D", "environmental scanning and customer knowledge" and "quality and assessment capabilities, and in-house training". These objectives are drivers for the objectives and measures in the internal processes perspective.

The vertical strategic themes describe the chain of cause-and-effect relationship between the drivers that will lead to the strategic outcomes and the desired outcomes. The strategy maps provide a logical way to communicate the organisation's desired outcomes and how these outcomes can be achieved. The linkages in strategy maps are based on the strategic themes and describe the cause-and-effect relationships for value creation over the planning horizon.

Turku Polytechnic has two vertical strategic themes that emphasise the outcomes in the customer perspective. The first theme emphasises the external impact of Turku Polytechnic on its region. The second theme focuses on the clusters of biotechnology, information and communication technology, metal and marine technology, which are the strengths of the local economy and where economic growth is expected. The third vertical strategic theme emphasises the capabilities and knowledge which can be used to develop the internal processes.

Figure 1. The strategy map of Turku Polytechnic

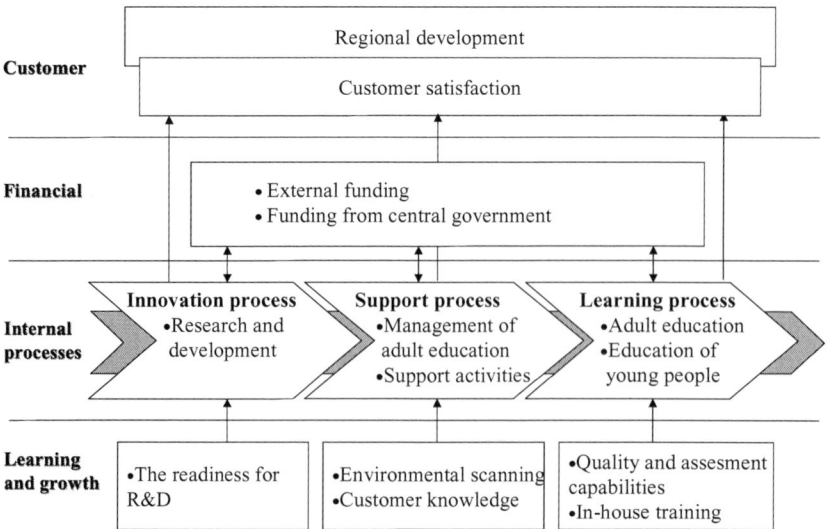

The horizontal strategic theme, which is connected with the value chain, describes the causal chain of value creation. The essence of the strategy is in the activities and it requires an "organisational theory" of value creation. The activities are embodied in the value chain, which can be described as the cooperation of different organisational units in the internal processes perspective.

Turku Polytechnic has one horizontal strategic theme, which emphasises that the results of research and development are used in education. The value chain is a description of the sequential process including research and development, support activities and education. In the long term the purpose is that research and development should provide results for high quality learning. In the medium term the purpose is to increase customer value through support activities and in the short term to achieve operational excellence in education.

The adult education at Turku Polytechnic can interpreted within the framework of the strategy map. The management of adult education is located in the support processes, but adult education is located in the learning process. This reflects the structure of the organisation, because the centre for continuing education and other support activities manage the continuing education, but the majority of the teachers in continuing education are from the education departments.

Environmental scanning and customer knowledge are required in the management of adult education. According to Peters (1988) the essence of strategy is the creation of organisational capabilities that will allow individuals to react opportunistically to whatever happens. Quality and assessment capabilities and in-house training are required to ensure high quality learning.

The results of research and development are widely used in adult education. Extensive management, planning, marketing and other support activities are needed to start the programmes. The long educational programmes are mainly funded by central government. Adult education aims to achieve customer satisfaction and have positive external impacts on its region.

5. The Balanced Scorecard for continuing education

Turku Polytechnic has nine education departments, ten shared support units and a continuing education centre. The support units provide services to help the departments manage their operations consistently with the strategy of Turku Polytechnic. The continuing education centre manages the continuing education and the education departments manage the degree programmes in adult education. Each of these departments has its own strategies and Balanced Scorecards.

The continuing education centre of Turku Polytechnic has selected the strategy of focus, which is combined with the strategy of cost efficiency. It builds long-term agreements and long-lasting customer relationships with the main organisations in Southwest Finland and serves these customers particularly well. On the other hand, the education is strongly linked to the strengths of the departments. New strategies have emerged from local initiatives and also within the organisation as emphasised by Minzberg (1987). The strategy helps the centre to meet the needs of the customer organisations and achieve low costs.

The focus strategy has been adjusted according to where the centre is in its life cycle. The centre was established gradually during the 1990s and it has passed its initial stage. Now it has 30 workers and anticipates some further growth. Therefore the strategy of profitable growth is preferred and the pure profitability strategy is left for the mature phase of its life cycle. According to its strategy the centre seeks new products for existing customers and new customers for existing products, and simultaneously enhances its financial performance.

The selection of strategy emphasises objectives and measures which support the strategy. Then the primary measures should be selected to describe the growth of the activities. The measures should indicate how extensive the continuing education is. The measures should also describe how well the organisation has succeeded in achieving the financial outcome.

O'Neil et al. (1999) have presented criteria to be used in selecting the measures. The measures should reflect the process of strategic planning. They have to be simple and easily understandable. They should be attainable in reasonable time. They should support comparisons to other HEIs. They should support organisational learning and continuous improvement. The indicators should be based on data collected on a regular basis and routinely applied in educational management.

Performance indicators may reveal a management problem: "If you can't measure it, you can't manage it." (Kaplan and Norton, 1996). Words are not sufficient to communicate the development, because words can be used to mean different things to different people. When the strategy and vision statements are translated into measures, they are clarified and communicated.

Table 1 describes the Balanced scorecard of the continuing education centre at Turku Polytechnic. It includes objectives, measures and targets in four perspectives 2003-2006. The targets of the measure are annually updated as a result of a negotiation between the senior management team and the departments.

The customer perspective includes the measure of customer satisfaction, which provides feedback from students and employers on how well the continuing education centre is doing. Research by Jones and Sasser (1995) has shown that only when customers rate their experience as extremely or completely satisfactory are they likely to continue with their behaviour. The target is to increase student satisfaction and keep it at a reasonably high level.

The financial perspective includes the measure of external funding. An increasing path of external funding is expected, which reflects the strategy of profitable growth. The financial perspective is an important measure for continuing education. It is, however, a secondary target, which is a prerequisite for high quality learning.

The internal processes perspective includes increasing activities in research and development, publications and continuing education. The increasing volume of these activities reflects the selected strategy aiming to growth.

The learning and growth perspective includes the increasing number of employers having postgraduate degrees and the number of employees in long-term training. Rucci, Kirn and Quinn (1998) studied the drivers of future performance. The analysis revealed how improvements in training and employees' understanding of the business led to better outcomes.

Table 1. The Balanced Scorecard for continuing education at Turku Polytechnic

Perspectives and objectives	Measures	2003	2004	2005	2006
Customer:					
• Student satisfaction	• Satisfaction of students on a scale 1-5, where 5 is highest	3.0	3.5	3.5	3.5
• Employer satisfaction	• Satisfaction of employers on a scale 1-5, where 5 is highest	3.5	3.5	3.5	3.5
Financial:					
• External funding	• External funding, 1000 €	2500	2600	2700	2800
Internal processes:					
• Volume of R&D	• Number of R&D projects	5	6	6	6
• Publications	• Number of publications in the own series	2	3	5	5
	• Number of published articles	6	6	10	10
• Volume of continuing education	• Number of days provided in continuing education, 1000	110	110	110	110
	• Number of participants in continuing education	5500	6000	6000	6000
Learning and growth:					
• Number of employees with postgraduate degrees	• Number of licentiates	1	1	2	2
	• Number of doctorates	1	1	2	2
• Number of employees in long-term education	• Number of postgraduate students	0	0	0	2

6. Conclusions

The development of the Balanced Scorecard is an iterative process that enables continuous improvement and enhancement. It is better to start and improve than wait for a perfect solution before the implementation of the strategy. The experience of Turku Polytechnic shows that organisational change does not happen at one point in time but is a continuous management process.

The scorecards were based on an agreement between each department and the senior management team of Turku Polytechnic. The former professional careers of the heads of departments were within a narrow subject or function. The challenge was to give the leaders of the departments and degree programmes a general management perspective and new management tools.

The Balanced Scorecard stimulated an intense management dialogue and helped to redefine the existing strategy. The Balanced Scorecard helped the central administration of the HEI to accomplish the strategic themes, objectives and measures on overall organisational and departmental levels. The Balanced Scorecard was also useful to the personnel, because it enhanced their understanding of strategy and the objectives.

The strategy of focus combined with cost efficiency was selected for the basis for the overall strategy at Turku Polytechnic. The strategic themes emphasise the external impact of the HEI on the region and its main clusters. On the other hand they reflect the operational excellence of the internal processes and the importance of learning.

The strategy of the continuing education centre needs to be rethought, because the centre is operating in a market-led environment. The strategy was redefined for profitable growth, because the centre still anticipates some growth and is approaching the mature phase of its life cycle. The Balanced Scorecard helped to communicate and implement the selected strategy.

References

Frigio, M.L. and K. Krumwiede (1999), Balanced Scorecard: A Rising Trend in Strategic Performance Measurement, Journal of Strategic Performance Measurement, February-March, 42-48.

Jones, T.O. and W.E. Sasser (1995), Why Satisfied Customers Defect, Harvard Business Review, November-December, 88-99.

Kaplan, R. and D. Norton (1992), The Balanced Scorecard: Measures That Drive Performance, Harvard Business Review, January-February, 71-79.

Kaplan, R. and D. Norton (1993), Putting the Balanced Scorecard to Work, Harvard Business Review, September-October, 134-147.

Kaplan, R. and D. Norton (1996), The Balanced Scorecard, Boston, Massachusetts: Harvard Business School Press.

Kaplan, R. and D. Norton (2001), The Strategy-Focused Organisation, Boston, Massachusetts: Harvard Business School Press.

Kettunen, J. (2002), Competitive Strategies in Higher Education, Journal of Institutional Research 11, 38-47.

Kettunen, J. (2003a), Strategic Evaluation of Institutions by Students in Higher Education, Perspectives: Policy and Practice in Higher Education 7, 14-18.

Kettunen, J. (2003b), The Length of Study of MBA Students, International Journal of Lifelong Education 22, 159-171.

Lingle, J.H. and W.A. Shieman (1996), From Balanced Scorecards to Strategic Gauges: Is Measurement Worth It? Management Review, March, 56-62.

Minzberg, H. (1987), Crafting Strategy, Harvard Business Review, July-August, 66-75.

O'Neil, H.F.Jr., E.M. Besimon, M.A. Diamond and M.R. Moore (1999), Designing and Implementing an Academic Scorecard, Change 31, 32-40.

Peters, T. (1988), Thriving on Chaos: A Handbook for Management Revolution, London, Macmillan.

Porter, M. (1990), The Competitive Advantage of Nations, London: Macmillan.

Porter, M. (1996), What is Strategy? Harvard Business Review, November-December, 61-78.

Rucci, A.J., S.P. Kirn and R.T. Quinn (1998), The Employee-Customer-Profit Chain at Sears, Harvard Business Review, January-February, 82-97.

Simons, R. (1995), Levers of Control: How Managers Use Innovative Control Systems to Drive Strategic Renewal, Boston: Harvard Business School Press, 47-55, 156.

Treacy M. and F. Wiersema (1995), The Discipline of Market Leaders: Choose Your Customers, Narrow Your Focus, Dominate Your Market, Reading, MA: Addison-Wesley.

West-Burnham, J. (1994), Strategy, Policy and Planning, In T. Bush and J. West-Burnham (eds.), The Principles of Educational Management, Harlow: Longman.

Wheale, J. (1991), Generating Income for Educational Institutions: A Business Planning Approach, London: Kogan Page.

Printed in Great Britain
by Amazon.co.uk, Ltd.,
Marston Gate.